Knock
Your
Socks
Off
Selling

Be sure to take a look at the books in AMACOM's
bestselling Knock Your Socks Off Service series too!

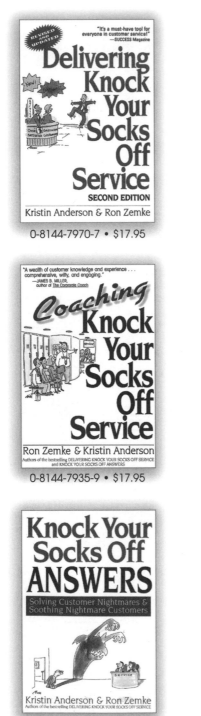

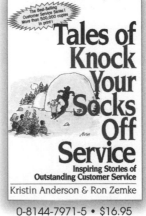

Knock Your Socks Off Selling

Jeffrey Gitomer
and Ron Zemke

AMACOM
American Management Association
New York • Atlanta • Boston • Chicago • Kansas City • San Francisco • Washington, D.C.
Brussels • Mexico City • Tokyo • Toronto

Library of Congress Cataloging-in-Publication Data

Gitomer, Jeffrey H.
    Knock your socks off selling / Jeffrey Gitomer and Ron Zemke.
        p.   cm.
    Includes bibliographical references (p.).
    ISBN 0-8144-7030-0
    1. Customer loyalty.   2. Consumer satisfaction.   3. Customer
services.   I. Zemke, Ron.   II. Title.
HF5415.525.G583   1999
658.85—dc21   99-18406
                                                          CIP

Printing number

10

Table of Contents

A Pair of Acknowledgments and Thank-Yous

From Jeffrey

When a work is completed, it's like a child was born. Another member of the family. I'm lucky; I love to write. So the pain of book-birth has eluded me—but the labor is clearly there.

A thank-you to my friend, editor, feedback mechanism, creative genius, and BS meter—Rod Smith—who has again provided his wisdom for this work. He labored hard to give the body of work a flow and defended the edits he made with his usual idealistic intransigence.

And a thank-you to my new friend and co-author Ron Zemke and his wonderful team—especially Jill Applegate—for their wisdom and support in maybe the first of many KYSO sales books. I am proud to be one of the Knock Your Socks Off authors.

And a HUGE thank-you to the readers of my weekly sales and customer service column, "Sales Moves." Their feedback has provided a wealth of inspiration and an eight-year steady flow of information from the real world of selling—America's primary business responsibility.

At this moment of my life, age 53, my family has taken on more of a primary role in my thoughts and actions. The children—Ericka, Stacey, and Rebecca are in full bloom. Married or engaged, working hard, and maturing into fine young women. A father's pride and inspiration. And the newest family additions—Morgan (of Rebecca) and Julia (of Stacey) are as beautiful to look at as their mothers.

My dad joined my mother this past year. His death was the hardest of realities. I will miss his wisdom and "sonny-boy, the old man is proud of you." What more could you wish to hear from your dad?

My new wife and lifemate, Teresa, is my daily support and reality check. I am so lucky to have found the person I was meant to be with.

I appreciate you and I thank you.

Jeffrey Gitomer
Salesman
Charlotte, NC
May 1999

From Ron

Books don't write themselves. Nor are they written exclusively by the people whose names appear on the cover. Not business books anyway. Sure, we the authors take full responsibility for what is, and isn't, here in black and white—and accept both blame and kudos where appropriate. But in a larger sense, this book is a product of the inspiration, encouragement, and wisdom of many, many people. Hank Kennedy, AMACOM's publisher, had the idea of a Knock Your Socks Off Selling book in the first place—and kept after it until we came to share the vision with him. Thanks, Hank. And thanks also to Ellen Kadin, Steve Arkin, and Irene Majuk who believed in this project as ardently and pushed as hard as Hank Kennedy to make it happen.

At the Minneapolis post, special thanks go to Jill Applegate, who kept the manuscript pages pouring—and in order (she deserves to be thanked twice); John Bush, whose art continues to adorn and punctuate the Knock Your Socks Off books and gives them a sense of visual style; partners Tom Connellan and Chip Bell who were always available for bouncing ideas back and forth; and of course, and always, Susan Zemke who can always find time in her busy practice to give a chapter, a paragraph, a phrase, or an idea her careful scrutiny and tender attention.

A very, very special thanks goes out to Helen Powers of Maryland Composition Company, Inc., in Glen Burnie, Maryland, who never flinched or batted an eye at our last-minute changes and whose watchful gaze kept those emergency, later-than-last-minute corrections, from creating a single disaster.

Most of all, we thank every customer, prospect, or suspect who has told us "yes," "no," or "maybe"— and made us learn to work to sell and serve them just that much better.

Ron Zemke
Minneapolis, MN
May 1999

Preface

Nothing Happens Until You Make It Happen

"I'll take it!"

Music to the ears of a salesperson. The problem is how to make that response happen more often than not.

Easy answer: Make the prospect like you, trust you, believe you, feel your value, and perceive a difference between you and your competition.

Easier answer: Knock Your Socks Off Selling!

The job of selling, more than any other, is surrounded with motivational slogans, airy aphorisms, and bumper sticker wisdom.

> *"Don't try to sell what you have"* rather *"have what people need and value."*
> *"It's not the $1,000 things that upset the customer, but the $5.00 things that bug them."*
> *"Treat each customer as an 'individual,' not a client."*
> *"It takes months to find a customer, seconds to lose one."*
> *"People don't buy goods, they buy solutions to problems."*

You've undoubtedly heard hundreds, if not thousands, of these one-sentence pep talks and sales seminar signposts. And though some of them—perhaps many of them—are oversimplified—even a little simpleminded—there is also a lot of truth and even more than a little wisdom in some of these motivational slogans. Like this one:

"Nothing Happens Until Somebody Sells Something"

For most of the 1990s, the focus of business has been on everything *but* selling. Branding. Positioning. Marketing. Partnering. Service. Innovation. Quality. Globalization. Internet. Technology. But as important as these ideas are to a business, none of them has the immediacy and impact on an organization's fate than the ageless act of selling; the act of going out, finding a prospect, and turning that prospect into a customer—someone who buys and uses and repurchases and reuses your products and services.

Now don't get us wrong! Great products and stunningly delivered services are critically important. Today's customer expects, make that *demands*, first-class products and flawless service. They are the price you pay to be a player in the game of

commerce today. But high-quality products and services alone won't make an organization—or you—successful. If that were all it took, there would be no need for salespeople at all. Business would simply be about creating and building, inventing and delivering. We would be living in a build-a-better-mousetrap world.

But we are not—far from it. We live in a world of intense competition for the customers' time, attention, and dollars. We live in an era of complex products and services. We live in an age where the subtle differences between products and services can perplex, confound, and elude a customer. We live at a time when the science of selling spells the difference between marketplace failure and marketplace domination; between organizations that become legendary and those that die an unhappy death.

We live in a world where the difference between the winners and also-rans is Knock Your Socks Off Selling.

Knock Your Socks Off Selling is about four things:

1. Finding qualified prospects,
2. Converting those prime prospects to customers,
3. Converting those customers to business partners, and
4. Maintaining positive, long-term relations with your customers/partners

The philosophy behind Knock Your Socks Off Selling is simple and straightforward; present your product to the right prospect in the right way, treat the prospect with respect and dignity, work to keep the customer happy with you and your product, and you will have a customer—if not for life—at least for a very long time. We believe the best customer relationships are those where the customer comes to see you almost as a partner in his or her business; someone who cares about the success of the customer's organization and feels a part of that success in some way.

This book is about the strategies, tactics, and techniques you need to understand and use to turn prospects into customers and customers into partners. This book is about the things you need to do to keep customers coming back again and again. This book is about building and maintaining long-term relationships. This book is about a commercial transaction called buying. And this book is about creating trust and respect between two people called buyer and seller.

But this book is also about you and the attitudes and mindset, tactics and techniques you must master to succeed at selling as a career. It is about the preparation, skill, and work it takes to make a sale and succeed with your customers.

This book is about what it takes to make you a Knock Your Socks Off Salesperson. And that is where this book belongs—with you—and with your determination to be the kind of salesperson who is willing to develop the discipline and have the skills that will make you a successful, positive, customer-focused salesperson.

The book is dedicated to the one thing salespeople need to make sales: ANSWERS.

It is with undying respect for the people who make things happen in business—the salespeople—that we give you *Knock Your Socks Off Selling*. A book that will put sales commissions where they belong. In your pocket.

Jeffrey Gitomer
Ron Zemke

Part One

Are You Ready for Knock Your Socks Off Selling?

When it's going well, nothing beats the exhilaration of selling for a living. Of turning a tough prospect into a happy customer. Of building a lasting relationship. Of being part of a great success story. Or earning the commission dollars you deserve.

But Is Knock Your Socks Off Selling for *you*? It's a fair question. Selling is a demanding profession. It isn't for everyone. Things don't always go well. For every yes you hear there are twenty no's and a dozen "so what"'s? and "I don't get it"'s. Customers aren't always nice, or respectful, or a joy to be around. And they

don't always say thank-you when you help them solve a problem or fix an error—even when they caused the problem in the first place. And sometimes the distance between Sale A and Sale B can seem an awfully long and twisted trail. Selling for a living is not for the faint of heart. Chapters 1 through 3 are your opportunity to answer three questions:

1. If so, what sort of a salesperson do I want to be?
2. Is Knock Your Socks Off Selling for me?
3. Where am I in my development as a sales professional?

1

The "Born" Salesperson

You've heard people say it. So have we:

"That Mike—why he's a born salesman."
"Wanda—Wow! She could sell an Alaskan a refrigerator!"

There are indeed people who are so good at sales that it just seems they have a special talent—a gift from God—that makes them so confident, so smooth, so easy with people, so facile with words, so competent and believable answering objections, so well, completely together, that they seem to validate the "Born Salesperson" belief with every move they make.

Guess what? There *are* born salespeople. Salespeople so good their companies wish they could clone them; so good their peers both envy them and believe in their heart of hearts that they could never emulate them. They are born all right—but not born of superior breeding or better genetic material or of parents determined to raise the world's greatest salesperson. No, they are born of the careful and painstaking work and study it takes to master the science of selling. Born of a determination to be the best, to make every opportunity count, to master every aspect of the most challenging person-to-person craft in the world—selling for a living.

These "born" salespeople come in both sexes, a variety of shades and sizes, every color and creed, and every conceivable combination of age and background. They are bright, average, and some more distinguished by tenacity than brilliance. They are well educated and not. They are introverts, extraverts, assertive, and shy. Their key commonality is their intense desire to succeed and their willingness to do whatever it takes to meet their goals.

Over the years, we have come to believe that there are some common everyday performance characteristics, skills, and developable attitudes and attributes that the "born" salesperson cultivates, develops, and hones. What follows is an inventory of twenty-one of these characteristics. Read through the list and decide whether it is a characteristic you exhibit or a habit you have developed, or a trait you possess. Decide "Yes" I have that trait or I have developed that habit or attitude or aptitude, or "No" I do not. Ok—we know that there can be a "middle ground" between "Yes" and "No." A place called "I'm working on it." Ignore that gray area and be a little hard on yourself—mark as a "No" those characteristics and skills you are working on but haven't mastered or fully developed to your own satisfaction. When you have worked through the list we will tell you how to score yourself. Take your time and think about each of the characteristics. Measure yourself honestly and carefully. No one but you will see your evaluation. There will be no grades, no winners, no losers. Just an opportunity to take a careful look at yourself and answer the question, "Am I on the road to becoming a *Knock Your Socks Off Salesperson*? Do I want to be?"

21 Characteristics of the "Born" Salesperson

Yes No

☐ ☐ **I have good self-discipline.** I can forgo a "good time" to do the work it takes to prepare a quality presentation to a prospect. The "scut work" doesn't put me off.

☐ ☐ **I am self-motivated.** I can keep myself involved and focused on a tough account. I can get myself "up" to do the tough things that pay off.

☐ ☐ **I constantly work on becoming more knowledgeable.** I allot time to learn more about my company's products, my customers' businesses, and developments in my industry.

☐ ☐ **I continually work on my relationship building skills.** I take courses and read books and articles on relationship building. I solicit feedback from others on my skill level.

☐ ☐ **I am self-confident.** I know that I can be a success at selling. I see a great future for myself. The skills I don't have, I can develop.

☐ ☐ **I like myself.** Hey, I am a pretty good person. I deserve to do well. I actually enjoy my own company!

☐ ☐ **I love people.** I enjoy the company of others. I really come alive in a group. I can get along well with almost anyone.

☐ ☐ **I love a challenge.** Face to face with a tough customer is really stimulating. So is trying to figure out exactly what will sell him on us.

☐ ☐ **I love to win.** Being the one who gets the order in a competitive situation. It pumps me up.

☐ ☐ **I can accept rejection with a positive attitude.** "No" and "we aren't interested" just mean I have to find a better way to tell my story.

Yes   No

❏   ❏   **I can handle details.** Crossing the T's and dotting the I's isn't my favorite thing, but I can get it done. I know that doing the details does make a difference.

❏   ❏   **I am loyal.** I stand up for my customers and for my company. It's particularly important for me to stick up for my customers.

❏   ❏   **I am enthusiastic.** I get a charge out of selling. I really like it, and it shows to my customers that I like what I do.

❏   ❏   **I am observant.** I can read my customers and my coworkers. I know when a presentation or an interview is going well. I can easily spot the signs.

❏   ❏   **I am a good listener.** I don't need to be the only one who talks. I know how to shut up and learn from my customers and my coworkers.

❏   ❏   **I am a skillful communicator.** I make persuasive presentations. I can keep people's attention when I talk. I'm good at back-and-forth conversations as well.

❏   ❏   **I am a hard worker.** I believe that hard work pays off, so I am willing to put in the hours.

❏   ❏   **I am perceptive.** I understand the subtleties of a situation. I can follow the drift of what is being said—and what is being left unsaid.

❏   ❏   **I have put my goals in writing.** I know exactly where I want to be next week, next month, and next year. And five years from now as well.

❏   ❏   **I am persistent.** I can take no for an answer, but I seldom do. An account that is worth having is worth keeping after. And I do.

❏   ❏   **I want to be financially sound.** Selling for a living is an opportunity to build financial security. I have a plan and I am working it. Now.

Scoring Instructions

Count up your yeses. Put the number here

If you answered "Yes" to fifteen or more of these characteristics, you are on your way to becoming one of those "born" salespeople.

If you said "Yes" to ten to fourteen characteristics, you are still in good shape. This is especially true if you said yes to the characteristics of enthusiasm, self-confidence, perception, self-motivation, and working to become more knowledgeable.

If you said "Yes" to fewer than ten of these characteristics, particularly if you said "No" to the characteristics of enthusiasm, self-confidence, perception, self-motivation, and the enthusiasm for learning, you have a considerable journey in front of you. It is possible that you can become one of the "Born Salespeople," but it is more likely your talents lie in another direction.

Notice something important about this list of success characteristics? It is a list of desires, basic aptitudes, and attitudes. It is *not* really a list of the technical skills of selling, skills like closing a sale or overcoming an objection. Those are skills that can be learned, learned by anyone who has the desire to succeed, a few basic aptitudes, and the fortitude and persistence necessary to acquire and use them.

RULE #1:

Successful selling is a learnable set of skills— for those with the fortitude, aptitude, and persistence to succeed.

There are no other rules.

2

The Fundamentals of the Knock Your Socks Off Sales Call:

How Do You Rate?

Some sales experts would have you think that there is a lock stop, "one best way" approach to making a sales call. We respectfully disagree. There are common elements to good selling. And there are some pretty effective ways of working toward a sale. But every salesperson executes the process and uses the fundamental elements in a different, personally unique way. Every great salesperson we've ever worked with has his or her own way of moving from "Hi, good to meet you" to "Thank you for your order."

Presented here—in the form of a self-assessment survey—are the 18.5 basic elements of a Knock Your Socks Off, face-to-face sales call. Are these 18.5 elements all-encompassing? Everything you'll ever need to know to be the best-ever salesperson in your company? Possibly not. But, if you've mastered these 18.5 fundamental elements, you *are* doing a great job. You are on your way to becoming a superb, first-rate, Knock Your Socks Off salesperson.

We are focusing here on the basic elements of the face-to-face sales call, even though we know full well there is a lot more to long-term success with customers than face-to-face selling and that not all selling is done face-to-face in the prospect's office or conference room. However, the face-to-face, in the customer's office, sales situation is the sine qua non of selling—the ultimate selling situation. It contains all the elements of every other type of selling—retail, over the phone, trade show—that you will ever encounter. It is the most pressure filled and personal of sales. It is the most dependent on creating that perfect balance between presenting tailored technical information and establishing a positive personal relationship. It requires great information-gathering skill, skillful conversation management, masterful questioning, marvelous presentation making, and superb practical objection handling. The face-to-face sales call has it all. Master the basics of the face-to-face sales call and you have mastered the basics of Knock Your Socks Off Selling—whether you sell face to face, over the phone, or over the counter.

As you read through and evaluate yourself on these fundamentals, you probably will notice that you already know and practice many of them. Remember, these are the fundamentals, the basics of Knock Your Socks Off Selling; just as serve and volley are the basics of tennis, drive and putt are the basics of golf, and block and tackle are the basics of football. They should feel familiar. And just as mastering those sports depends on mastering the basics, you, as a salesperson, can't progress to the more sophisticated and—dare we say—sexier elements of Knock Your Socks Off Selling until the selling game's fundamentals are a smooth and polished part of your selling repertoire, your everyday performance.

Assessing Yourself on the Basics

What follows is a listing and brief explanation of the 18.5 fundamentals of a Knock Your Socks Off sales call. The objective here is evaluative, not instructional—although most people learn a lot about selling just from doing this assessment. Just the same, don't be concerned if you rate yourself low in a specific area and can't immediately see what you can do to improve— that's what the rest of the book is about; the things you can do to improve your basic selling skills.

To make the most of this assessment, be ruthlessly honest and candidly critical of yourself and your current level of selling skills. If you are, two things will happen. First, you will see places where you need improvement; areas of your sales call performance that can profit from a plan of study and improvement. Second, you will be delighted at how good you already are in other areas; skills you have that you weren't really conscious of, had never though much about, and where you already are a Knock Your Socks Off performer.

Here's how it works:

1. Read each statement through completely twice.
2. Think about a time that the statement was true of you on a sales call—true is good in this assessment.
3. Then think about a time when the statement was not true of you on a sales call.
4. Once you have these two instances in mind, ask yourself the critical question: "On balance, is the statement more true of my day-to-day selling or is it less frequently true of my efforts than it should be?"
5. When you've decided, circle a number on the 1 to 9 scale underneath the statement that describes how good your day-to-day execution of that fundamental is right now. There is a place at the end of the assessment for tabulating and evaluating the results.

1 ------- 2 ------- 3 ------- 4 ------- 5 ------- 6 ------- 7 ------- 8 ------- 9

This is seldom true of me	This is sometimes true of me	This is how I operate all the time

1. **I know the prospect and his or her business before I walk in the door.** When I walk into a prospect's office, I know a lot more than his or her name, title, and the company name. I know at least four out of five of the following:

   - Who the prospect currently is purchasing my type of product or service from.
   - Whether the prospect has sole authority to purchase from us or whether purchasing decisions are a committee decision.
   - Whether anyone from my company has called on this prospect before.
   - Whether the prospect ever bought from us before and, if so, why he or she didn't continue to purchase from us.
   - How long the prospect has been with his or her company.

   I believe that walking into a prospect's office knowing less than this is disrespectful and a sure route to a very short appointment.

This is seldom   This is sometimes   This is how I
true of me   true of me   operate all the time

2. I always know when I am talking to a decision maker.
It is both disrespectful and a waste of everyone's time
meeting with someone who has no interest in my product or service or who has no responsibility or authority to
make a purchase from me.

Caveat: I understand that today there is a lot of committee decision making around the purchase of high-
dollar or highly complex systems and services. In that
instance, I expect to be talking with a lot of people
about my product or service. I work to not be in the position of being represented to others on the buying
team by a single person. I try to get to everyone on the
decision-making team. I know that, at a minimum, I
need to talk to three people on a four-person decision-
making team.

I make every effort to be in the room when the decision
is made if I can't present to the final decision maker
myself.

This is seldom   This is sometimes   This is how I
true of me   true of me   operate all the time

3. **I approach the prospect with friendliness and confidence.** I understand that first impressions are lasting impressions. I also understand that phoniness almost never works. Children, dogs, and prospects know when you are faking it. I try to be the most confident, self-assured, and friendly me I can be.

   I understand that people buy from people they are comfortable with, and they are more comfortable with friendly people. I also believe that people buy from people who have gained their confidence—people who send signals of knowing what they are talking about and of being comfortable in the prospect's presence.

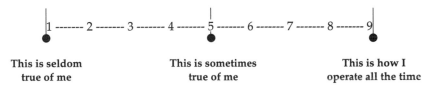

This is seldom   This is sometimes   This is how I
true of me   true of me   operate all the time

4. **I know—and know how to find out—the prospect's true wants and needs.** My ironclad rule, especially for first calls on a prospect, is "Question first. Tell second." I wouldn't think of starting a second or third or eighth visit with a prospect or customer without reviewing—via questioning—all that has gone before. It refreshes the understanding of both parties. I believe it is important to learn everything I can from—and about—a prospect or customer.

Most important is using the first moments of the first meeting—once amenities are out of the way; the prospect knows who you are and who your company is—learning from the prospect, not telling. Learning means asking questions that reveal the prospect's needs and wants. Questioning a prospect—without seeming to be interrogating him or her—is a skill we will discuss later.

This is seldom	This is sometimes	This is how I
true of me	true of me	operate all the time

5. **I show the prospect that I care about him or her personally.** I talk to the prospect in terms of his and his company's needs. I offer a specific plan or scenario as to how our product or service will impact his business. I show empathy for his point of view when it differs from mine. I am respectful of the prospect's beliefs and views even when I disagree with them or know them to be wrong. If I have to tell a prospect he or she is wrong, I can do so tactfully.

This is seldom	This is sometimes	This is how I
true of me	true of me	operate all the time

6. I know how to ask drop-dead questions. I know how to build a prospect's confidence in me and my organization through the questions I ask. I ask questions that help both of us see what will best help the prospect's organization—and create a positive buying atmosphere. I have learned how to ask questions that help the prospect see things in a new or different light. I spend time thinking about and developing good questions.

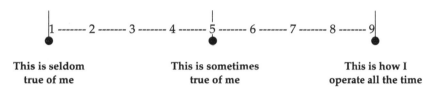

This is seldom   This is sometimes   This is how I
true of me   true of me   operate all the time

7. I can show the prospect how my product or service is used—not just what it does. I know that the prospect is only marginally concerned with the features and technology of my product or service. I understand that the real concern is what my product or service can do for the prospect personally or for his or her organization. I know how to sell the benefits of using our products and/or services. I know our products very well and am almost never stumped by a technical question. When I am unsure about product performance, I can find out immediately.

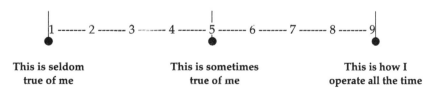

This is seldom   This is sometimes   This is how I
true of me   true of me   operate all the time

8. I can present a compelling message. I know that my ability to speak well is as important as my ability to present my case clearly. I try to motivate the prospect by appealing to both noble and course buying motives (e.g., quality, reliability, vanity, fear, etc.). I can paint a work picture of the benefits of using the products and what it would feel like to be a customer.

This is seldom   This is sometimes   This is how I
true of me   true of me   operate all the time

9. I make sure the prospect is paying close attention. I work at keeping all distractions away from the presentation space—including my own company materials, proposal summaries, and other tabletop distractions. Where possible, I get the prospect out of his or her office, and off site, where the odds are lowest of an emergency phone call or walk-in interruption. I can see and sense the signs of inattention and boredom, and I know how to deal with them. I believe in keeping my presentations short, clear, and direct.

This is seldom   This is sometimes   This is how I
true of me   true of me   operate all the time

10. I know how to make the prospect feel important. I ask for the prospect's opinion and input. I compliment the prospect for his or her success, acumen, and prior good decisions. I understand there is a big difference between vacant flattery and demonstrating that I know the prospect's position in, and importance to, his or her organization. I frequently ask the prospect for guidance in influencing others on the buying team. I respect my older customers' experience and wisdom and admire the success, spirit, and achievements of my younger prospects.

This is seldom   This is sometimes   This is how I
true of me   true of me   operate all the time

11. I routinely tell stories that emphasize a point or tie into my message. I believe in telling stories that help the prospect visualize results and ownership. Facts are usually pretty boring; stories are interesting. Facts are forgotten; stories are retold. I understand that stories are more powerful and memorable than are statistics and data. I believe stories help the prospect visualize the results of owning our product or using our service. I am constantly on the lookout for new stories.

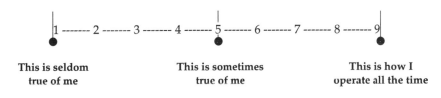

This is seldom   This is sometimes   This is how I
true of me   true of me   operate all the time

12. I can make powerful proof statements that give the prospect confidence. In my presentations, I emphasize how our products or services have helped others—by name. I show how they have used them to their benefit. I routinely ask existing customers for testimonials about the performance of our products or services and use these in my presentation. I keep on top of the new applications both my customers and the company develop for our products.

This is seldom   This is sometimes   This is how I
true of me   true of me   operate all the time

13. I can overcome objections and statements of doubt with questions—not just statements. I avoid fast comebacks to objections and doubts. I know that seems too pat and can create more doubt. I know how to ask questions that help the prospect overcome his own objections. I understand and believe that objections are buying signals. I see an objection as a prospect's request for more information.

This is seldom   This is sometimes   This is how I
true of me   true of me   operate all the time

14. I routinely use testimonials as final proof. I avoid using them as door openers. I know the prospect expects proof of what I say. The best proof I can use is the words of other customers. I use my testimonials and proof statements to close—not open—the sales presentation. I keep a trove of testimonials available to use in the selling process. I keep my testimonial files fresh and up to date. I would not hesitate to call an existing customer from a prospect's office and ask him or her to speak candidly of our product or service.

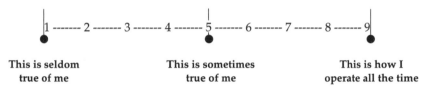

This is seldom   This is sometimes   This is how I
  true of me   true of me   operate all the time

15. I look for signals of trust from the prospect. I know the trust between buyer and seller is key to any long-term relationship. I look for signs of trust, such as asking my advice, looking me in the eye when we talk, and seeking my reassurance. I believe that knowing the customer's expectations and working to keep both implicit and explicit promises made to my customer is the best way of earning a customer's confidence.

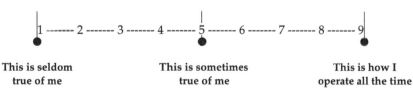

This is seldom   This is sometimes   This is how I
  true of me   true of me   operate all the time

16. I seek to gain agreement from the prospect. Gaining agreement throughout the sales process is important. I ask easy-to-agree-with questions as I go: "Do you see what I mean?," "Do you see how this fits with your needs?," "Do you see how this might impact your organization?" I believe that closing a sale is a process, not an event. The phrase A-B-C "Always Be Selling" is true of my approach to selling.

| This is seldom | This is sometimes | This is how I |
| true of me | true of me | operate all the time |

17. I make it a point to ask for the sale. It is important to actually ask for the sale. I ask several times during the process. I know that asking for the business doesn't offend the prospect—it's expected. I realize that a "no" isn't necessarily final, but I work to make it easy for my prospects to say "yes."

| This is seldom | This is sometimes | This is how I |
| true of me | true of me | operate all the time |

18. I can close the sale, get agreement on the next action, and make sure that I get out before my welcome is worn out. This is the final agreement. I understand that the key is mutual agreement on the next action. I know that the agreement must be a solid one—or I don't leave. I know how to close a sale and get agreement on next steps. I know how to confirm that the sale is truly made. I also know when it is time to depart.

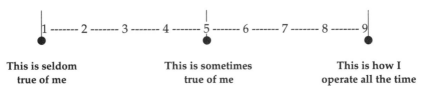

This is seldom   This is sometimes   This is how I
true of me   true of me   operate all the time

18.5. I am friendly. Occasionally funny, always relaxed, and always sincere. I know that the tone I set for the face-to-face meeting is important. I believe that being friendly, relaxed, sincere—and occasionally funny—is a good tone for a sales meeting. I state my purpose for the presentation at the outset, then work at setting the tone of the meeting.

This is seldom   This is sometimes   This is how I
true of me   true of me   operate all the time

Scoring Instructions

1. Go back through these 18.5 items and add up your score. Put the results here:

2. The maximum score possible is 181 points. Here are some rule-of-thumb ranges and their interpretations you can use to assess your overall score.

   19–66:   You have a lot of work to do. Your prospect's socks are in danger of disintegrating. Were you being too tough on yourself?

   67–123:   You are doing ok. There are areas to work on, but you are getting the idea of Socks Off Selling.

   124–162: You're making a move. You obviously have a lot of barefooted but happy customers. Good work!

   163–171: Wow! Scores like this Knock *Our* Socks Off! Are you sure you aren't being a little generous with yourself?

3. Go back once again and look for items on which you gave yourself a 5 or lower. Write those items in the spaces below. (If there are more than half a dozen, just record the five items with the lowest scores.)

   • _____

   • _____

   • _____

- _____

- _____

Is there a pattern here? Are the low scores about prepa-ration? Presentation making? Questioning skills?

4. Take a 3" x 5" notecard. Label one side "Strengths" and the other side "Improvements." On the "Strengths" side, write the five factors you rated yourself *highest* on. On the "Improvements" side, list the five factors you need to work on.

Keep the card where you can refer to it. We will come back to the list frequently in the final section of the book.

3

Is the Consultative Approach to Knock Your Socks Off Selling for You?

There are salespeople—and there are salespeople. Not every one sells with the same ends in mind or from the same philosophy. There are two major approaches to selling you should consider; two ways of looking at the job of salesperson.

- One is the **sales rep** approach, which is characterized by finding prospects and making presentations.
- The other approach is **consultative selling**, which is characterized by uncovering needs, building relationships, and solving problem for customers. Consultative selling is at the heart of the Knock Your Socks Off Selling philosophy. Whether you choose to follow that path is a personal decision—and one you should consider seriously.

What follows is a more detailed explanation of these two approaches and an evaluation you can use for determining which approach fits your temperament and goals best.

The Sales Rep Approach

A sales rep is someone who walks into a customer's or prospect's office ready, willing, and able to extol the virtues of a product or service—given just half a chance. Equipped and able to explain the features and benefits and show the advantages of using Acme's products or services over those of the competition. The sales rep's plea is "Mr. Prospect, give me a minute to introduce you to the Acme Inc. and I know you'll be impressed." It is a time-tested, tried and true approach to selling. The straight-ahead, sales rep approach to selling revolves about the idea that by persuasively presenting your product or service in the best possible light, the customer or prospect will buy from you. Nothing wrong with the approach; it is relevant and useful in a number of situations. Telemarketers, retail store sales associates, and even many automobile and insurance salespeople sell that way all the time.

A sales rep's success depends on three things:

1. Mastering the sales basics (described in the assessment in the last chapter)
2. Knowing the company's products and services inside out
3. Getting in front of qualified prospects and customers—people the sales rep can *assume* to have a need for his or her products and/or services—as often as possible with a smooth, well-practiced presentation; a clean and polished presentation that varies little from customer to customer

The sales rep approach to selling is a numbers game. Get yourself a hearing from enough people, and you will succeed. In the early 1980s, Ron Zemke's company Performance Research Associates was involved in a study of successful sales reps for a Fortune 500 office machine manufacturer. The question to be researched: What do the top 20 percent of our sales reps do differently from our average sales rep? To answer the question, a research team went on 3,000 sales calls with 800 salespeople. One of the most important things learned was that the elite 20 percent, the significantly better-performing sales reps, made more calls than the *average* sales rep. Specifically, the high performers averaged *one-half sales call per day* more—that comes to 2.5 per week and 125 per year—than the average sales rep.

The sales rep approach is great for selling simple products or when the selling process is very straightforward. A good many people make a very nice living following the sales rep approach and way of thinking. Retail selling is, basically, sales rep selling. So are telemarketing and the sales of a number of business-to-business commodities such as building maintenance, perishables, and most office supplies. Sometimes, however, there is a need for a more involved sales process.

The Consultative Approach to Selling

Consultative selling is a more complex, involved approach to selling than is sales rep selling. It is a vital and important approach in situations and businesses where the product or service being sold is highly complex and/or where a long-term relationship is key to profitability of an account. Consultative selling is a necessity for selling to large companies, where millions of dollars are invested in a single sale and where annual renewals are part of the process. Consultative selling is at the very heart of Knock Your Socks Off Selling in:

- **Industrial sales.** Where the cost of establishing an account is high and profitability improves over the life of the account.
- **Life insurance.** Where customers can easily cancel their policies and move to another provider, and account profitability increases over the life of the policies held.
- **High technology.** Where applications are tailored to customers' specific needs and sales have a very long cycle; that is, it takes a long time to make a sale, often months, occasionally years.
- **Business and personal services.** Where customers can opt for another provider at any time or at least at some regular point in time. Health maintenance organization and healthcare contracts are open for reconsideration on a regular basis.

The consultative approach is customer and problem centered and not product or service centered. Consultative salespeople are known more by the questions they ask than by the sparkling presentations they make. The consultative salesperson is in the business of understanding a prospect's needs and problems, and proposing solutions that entail the use of the salesperson's products and/or services, yes, but frequently the products and services of others as well.

Although it is true that the consultative salesperson makes calls and sales presentations just like the sales rep, there is a difference in the amount of preparation and kind of follow-up that surround those sales calls and presentations. And there are differences in the attitude, the approach, and the commitment to building an account over time, rather than making a quick, one-time sale.

- **A consultative salesperson** is willing to forgo short-term gains to achieve greater long-term benefit for himself and the customer he serves.
- **A consultative salesperson** builds a one-to-one relationship on a foundation of trust, respect, and performance.
- **A consultative salesperson** gains and builds credibility. That credibility comes from consistently demonstrating preparedness, knowledge, expertise, and genuine concern for the customer's success in a way that is perceived by the customer to be useful, needed, and valuable.

In short, the consultative salesperson is viewed as a resource *in the mind of the prospect*.

Still unsure about the differences between "sales repping" and being a "consultative salesperson?" Not yet sure that the difference isn't simply a matter of semantics or word play? Figure 1 contains ten couplets or pairs of statements that differentiate consultative and sales rep thinking, attitudes, and behaviors.

Figure 1.

Consultative Selling vs. Sales Rep Selling

Consultative Selling	Sales Rep Selling
• Consultants think long term.	• Sales reps think short term.
• Consultants are considered experts.	• Sales reps are considered vendor representatives.
• Consultants don't sell. They make recommendations that help the prospect to buy.	• Sales reps position, present, and close. They sell, sell, sell.
• Consultants are confident.	• Sales reps fight to gain a positive image.
• Consultants are articulate and thoughtful.	• Sales reps are fast talkers.
• Consultants are considered resources and sought out and listened to.	• Sales reps are used as needed.
• Consultants are problem solvers.	• Sales reps tell about their products.
• Consultants ask probing questions.	• Sales reps ask leading questions.
• Consultants are friends, mentors, and advisors to buyers.	• Sales reps want to make sales—not manage relationships.
• Consultants offer solutions to important business or personal problems.	• Sales reps overcome objections and close sales.
• Consultants are highly paid professionals.	• Sales reps are commission-focused workers.
• Consultants think, "How can I help?"	• Sales reps think, "What can I push?"
• Consultants want to know more about helping.	• Sales reps want to know more about closing.
• Consultants are positioned in the client's mind as a resource-providing value.	• The Sales rep's core value is in the products and services he or she has available.

If the characteristics of the consultative salesperson appeal to you, you've taken the first step. You have an affinity for the Knock Your Socks Off approach and consultative selling.

CAUTION: Becoming a consultative salesperson isn't something you achieve overnight, something you simply pronounce yourself to be. It's a dedicated self-discipline that must be practiced every day. It is not just a dedication to changing the way you think about selling, but a dedication to changing and enhancing the way you think about yourself and your customers.

> **KYSO TIP:**
> Thinking of yourself as a consultant is one thing. Having the customer perceive you as one is quite another. To change titles, you must change the commitment you make.

Who golfs more Ned, Sales reps or consultants?

4

The Five Commitments of Consultative Knock Your Socks Off Selling

At its core, the consultative Knock Your Socks Off Selling approach has five important components. Three of them are the heart of what you do in consultative selling that distinguishes you from a sales rep, and two are about your attitude toward your organization and what your products and services can do for a customer. They all are *commitments* you make to yourself and your customers.

1. **Finding and understanding the customer's needs.** The sales rep focuses on finding qualified prospects—people who should have a need for his or her products—and persuading those qualified prospects to give the rep a hearing. The consultative salesperson has the same task—plus. Once the consultative salesperson has found a prospect, the job changes.

   Through questions and dialogue, the consultative salesperson must uncover the problem the customer is trying to solve or the need he or she is trying to meet—that has some relation to the salesperson's products and services. The core commitment, however, is to meet a need or solve a problem that is important to the customer, not a single-minded commitment to the product or service. Consultative salespeople often ask themselves and their company, "How can we reengineer what we make (or do) to better meet this customer's needs?"

2. **Partnering with the customer.** Once the problem to be solved or need to be met is identified, the consultative salesperson's detective work isn't finished. The salesperson must find a way to convince the prospect to allow him or her to become a partner—an ally—in coming up with a solution to the problem.

   This means that the Knock Your Socks Off sales consultant must focus first and foremost on how the need can be met most effectively and efficiently. Occasionally, this can entail helping the customer come up with a plan that has only a small benefit to a salesperson. Why would a salesperson go to all that trouble for only a little piece of the action? Simple. The consultative salesperson believes that, in the long term, his or her role as an advice giver and problem-solving partner is more valuable than a single sale. The consultative salesperson is committed to building long-term, positive relationships.

3. **Helping customers achieve their business objectives.** Consultative selling has an element of faith and trust in it. There is an implicit belief on the part of the consultative salesperson that if he or she is seen as not just selling, but as helping the customer meet his or her business needs, the customer will bring business to the salesperson. Does this quid quo pro always work out? No. There are indeed customers who aren't fair and who see no obligation to the salesperson who puts the customer's needs first. They use your time and your advice and buy from someone else—usually a low-price, no-service provider. But they are a rare breed. Both of us have had a prospect come back to us after years of virtually free advice and counsel and become a 1-A high-profit customer. Call it "The Law of Psychological Reciprocity" applied to selling. People you do good for are happy to do good things for you. Good deeds do indeed pay off.

And there is one other aspect to consider: how it feels to exchange favors as well as business. Our colleague, Dr. Chip Bell, does a lot of work with the Marriott organization. When he travels, he insists on staying in Marriott hotels, even when working for another client. Why? "They trust me to give them good advice. The least I can do is trust them to give me a good night's sleep. It wouldn't feel right if I didn't." Consultative salespeople are committed to a positive, reciprocal, back-and-forth relationship with customers.

4. **Believing that your products and service are a great fit with your customer's needs.** It's hard to be a salesperson if you don't believe in your products and services. A friend of ours, let's call her Laura, worked for a company that sold household items via infomercials and toll-free in-bound telephone service. Laura's instructions were whenever a customer called to complain about a product failure, she was to immediately offer to replace the item—to ship a new one without waiting for the old one to be shipped back. In fact, she could, if the product sounded to be in bad shape, ask the customer to simply

throw it out. Great service? That's what Laura thought—until someone clued her in. It turned out that several of the products the company sold were borderline hazardous: lamps that shorted out, chairs that tipped over a bit too easily. The company was trying to avoid lawsuits—and betting that the majority of buyers would simply not bother to complain when a product failed. Laura lasted six weeks. "I just couldn't sit there and represent a shoddy product—it was too hard on my nerves—and my heart," she told us. Fortunately, the company is no longer in business.

It is fundamental to the consultative Knock Your Socks Off approach that your products and services are capable of solving customer problems and meeting customer needs, that they have a price, performance quality, or value advantage you are more than willing to present, stand behind, and advocate—when the time is right. Pride and confidence in your company and its products and service is something your customers can read in your eyes and hear in your voice. It is a confidence you can't fake. Consultative salespeople are committed to providing their customers with top-notch products and services.

5. **Believing in yourself and your ability to help customers solve their problems.** Here's the critical difference between the sales rep and the consultative salesperson: the ability and willingness to help customers solve problems. It means knowing more than just your products and services. It means knowing how your products and services will fit into the customer's organization, and what are the strengths and limitations of your product and the competition's products. It means being willing and able to set a prospect right when he or she is buying your product for a use for which it is not suited.

Being a consultative salesperson means knowing the industry, the trends, the newest techniques, and the latest applications. It means being a resource for alternative ways to solve the same problem—and knowing the pluses and minuses of those alternatives. Being a consultative salesperson means being committed to the customer's needs and problems first and your own second. Being a Knock Your Socks Off salesperson means having a passion for what your customer does and having a commitment to being a partner in the customer's success.

Part Two

The Fundamentals of Knock Your Socks Off Selling

Finding prospects and turning them into customers. That's the goal. But in today's complex, time-pressed, competitive marketplace, it takes sophisticated strategies, processes, and tactics to get that job done. Finding your way through the tangle and thicket of dead ends, false starts, and "no thank-you's" takes a well-equipped hardy soul.

The winner, the Knock Your Socks Off salesperson, is, inevitably, the one who studies and masters the fundamentals and hones them to a sharp edge through practice, discipline, and self-study.

5

Cold Calling:

Creating Prospects the Hard Way

The cold call—trying to interest someone you don't know, and who doesn't know you, into talking to you about your products or services—is as tough as it gets in selling. In telemarketing, for example, where cold calling is a way of life, turnover due to burnout routinely runs over 100 percent a year.

Calling on existing customers is a lot more fun. They know you. They like you. They treat you nice. They offer you coffee. They've sent you money. If you talk to them nicely they'll probably send you more. It's a little like going home to see the friends and relatives. You're accepted.

Anyone with an ounce of empathy can understand why most salespeople are reluctant to pick up the phone or walk into an unfamiliar office and say, "Hello, my name is Jeffrey and I'm from Acme Widgets. I'd like to talk to the person in charge of widget buying."

Ninety percent of that time—that's nine times out of ten—cold calling or cold canvassing a "suspect" (someone you think might turn into a prospect, but aren't sure about yet) will turn into a turn down. They will say "no." They will say, "we are happy with the widget supplier we have now. Goodbye." Sometimes they'll just hang up. Sometimes they'll just point to a sign on the wall of the reception area that says "NO SOLICITATION" or even the friendlier "ABSOLUTELY NO SOLICITATION!"

So Why Bother?

Good question! You bother because there *are* people out there who will turn into prospects and then into customers—if you can reach them and give them a chance.

Performance Research Associates has done many, many customer satisfaction studies over the last ten years and routinely finds that 10 to 15 percent of an organization's current customers are actively looking for a new vendor, and that 20 to 30 percent more are "at risk," very willing to listen to someone who can promise better product, cheaper product, better delivery, or superior service.

Percentage of Customers	Satisfaction Rating
10–15%	Extremely satisfied
40–60%	Satisfied
20–30%	At risk
10–15%	Actively seeking a new vendor

The simple truth is that cold calling pays—it is one of the only ways for salespeople to uncover new, previously unsuspected prospects, people who are unhappy with their current situation or at least willing to listen to a better offer.

> **KYSO TIP:**
> Cold calling teaches you that you don't get great at sales in a day, you get great at sales day by day.

The Cold Facts About Cold Calling

There are, however, some cold hard facts that go with the promise of cold calling.

- Cold calls are, at best, a paradox. Cold calling is the hardest way to make a sale, so, of course, the newest salespeople are assigned to them—like some sort of fraternity initiation.
- For a mature, seasoned salesperson, cold calling is often a waste of time. If you have been in sales for more than five years, you should never be making cold calls.
- The cold call isn't—in fact—a way to make sales, it is a way to book an appointment to qualify a suspect as a prospect.

However,

- Cold calling is the best learning laboratory a salesperson could ever find.

Once you understand these facts of the cold calling life, you will see why we preach the fail-your-way-to-success approach to cold calling.

Fail-Your-Way-to-Success Cold Calling

Because the odds of a sale are low, because the best outcome of cold calling is an opportunity to make a call on a prospect, and because cold calling is a relatively anonymous activity (do you remember the name of one person who has cold called you by phone at dinner time?), it is a marvelous and safe way to hone your skills through practice, practice, practice!

Here's how to get great at selling by failing at cold calling.

- Identify the skills you want to practice.
- Dedicate an hour or two a day to learn and understand that it's not about making a sale—it's about learning how to sell.

With that mind-set you don't mind rejection, because it's part of the learning process—and, as you improve, occasionally you'll get paid for learning.

- Select one skill you want to perfect—let's say finding out who the widget-buying decision maker is in as many companies as you can in one day—then make ten calls, and goal yourself to get in to see or through to talk to five.

Following is a list of the 12.5 lifetime sales skills you can develop through the fail-your-way-to-success method of cold calling:

1. **Develop a fast opening that grabs attention and gets you to the next step.** What can you invent that gets immediate attention? Something that creates a smile—gets you in the door and gives you that 30-second opportunity with Mr. Big. What can you create that's innovative and gets you listened to every time? *Long-term benefit*: Teaches you to get to the point faster in your face-to-face presentations.

2. **Build instant rapport.** How fast can you put the other person at ease? How quickly can you get them to warm up to you? *Long-term benefit:* Teaches you that rapport is

the jumping-off point to begin the sale. The faster you can gain it, the smoother your path to sales success.

3. **Gain acceptance.** Being seen as a real person. Having your words believed. *Long-term benefit*: Teaches you that rapport leads to acceptance—if I like you, I'm more likely to accept what you say. The cold call leaves very little time to gain acceptance.

4. **Find the decision maker.** Being in front of someone who can say "yes" to you. Too many salespeople give a great sales presentation to the wrong person. *Long-term benefit*: Teaches you that selling the non-decision maker leads to a lifetime of fast-food drive-through windows; makes you more discerning with your efforts.

5. **Qualify the decision maker.** Finding out if the decision maker has the need and/or money to buy what you sell. *Long-term benefit:* Teaches you to be certain you're speaking to someone who can buy AND will spend. (CAUTION: "qualifying" is not to be mistaken for its evil twin—"pre-judging.") Qualifying simply means determining the potential value of a prospect. Is there a need? Is it imminent? Is the person you are talking to in a position to both say "yes" and authorize a purchase?

6. **Learn the power of questioning.** Being able to ask questions that make the prospect think and evaluate new information, and that separate you from your competition. *Long-term benefit*: Teaches you that asking questions about *them* leads to answers about *you—and your products and services*—and that leads to sales.

7. **Gain prospect interest.** Having useful information and ideas. Having information about the market and your ability to make your prospect's business grow and profit. *Long-term benefit*: Teaches you that the ability to gain the prospect's interest in your product or service stems from

your interest in the prospect's company, products and services, and problems and needs.

8. **Fast persuasion.** Getting others to say "yes" in a short period of time takes talent that only can be developed by practice. *Long-term benefit*: Teaches you to practice, and be effective, at presenting a compelling message and asking for the order.

9. **Persistence—the breakfast of winners.** The cold call usually will not generate a sale. It will generate a follow-up opportunity. *Long-term benefit:* Teaches you that most sales are made after the seventh "no" or, better stated, the seventh follow-up. Your persistence is in direct proportion to your level of success.

10. **Think on your feet.** You've got tops—30 seconds to figure it out—cold calls are not about fast-talking—they're about fast thinking. *Long-term benefit*: Teaches you to "think solution" and "think question," instead of spewing out a bunch of facts and figures that will be forgotten two seconds after the door has let you out of his office.

11. **The value of (and need for) creativity.** Cold calls are all about creativity. The opening line. The gatekeeper block. The decision-maker treasure hunt. The sale. The cool part about creativity is that it can be studied, learned, and practiced. *Long-term benefit*: Teaches you that creativity (which leads to memorability) is at the core of your sales success. The more creative you become, the easier it is to differentiate yourself from the dreaded competition (and their dreaded price).

12. **The joy of rejection.** Most people take rejection as a negative. It is, in fact, "the pathway to yes." Try this. Add a dose of humor to rejection. For example, start thanking people for telling you "no". Tell the prospect that only one out of four people buy—ask them if they know anyone else who might not be interested, because you still

need three more "no"'s before someone says "yes." It'll blow them away, and it'll make them laugh. Humor. Make me laugh and you can make me buy. The problem with rejection is that most people take it personally—big mistake. Prospects are not rejecting you as a person. They don't even know you as a person. They're just rejecting the offer you're making them. That feels better now, doesn't it? *Long-term benefit*: Teaches you that rejection is part of the success of selling. The more you can learn about why a prospect rejected you, the easier it is to eliminate the next rejection.

12.5. **It tells you if selling is for you.** If you can find the fun of cold calling and view it as the fail-your-way-to-success method to sales mastery, you ultimately will succeed at sales. If you can't, sales may not be your best career choice. *Long-term benefit*: Teaches you to do something you love, have the attitude to have fun at it, and dedicate yourself to be the best at it by learning something new every day.

Beyond Skill Practice

Cold calling will do two vital things for you. First, it *will* generate some bona fide prospect leads. Second, it will teach you an attitude that is irreplaceable. Beyond the skills you develop, cold calling will teach you to:

- **Be ready.** Cold calling teaches you the value of every second a prospect affords you.
- **Be creative.** Cold calling teaches you to be flexible and fluid in your approach to people. The more people you call, the more ways to find to present your arguments. One size does not fit all.
- **Be fast.** Cold calling teaches you to make your presentation concise, appealing, clear, and simple.
- **Have fun.** Cold calling teaches you to be loose, to be relaxed, and to chain and entertain prospects.

Hanging Tough When Call Reluctance Sets In

There are two brands of call reluctance. One is reluctance to pick up the telephone and call a prospect. The other is reluctance to make or ask for an appointment. Just to keep things straight, let's call one **telephone reluctance** and the other **appointment reluctance**. Both have similar origins and solutions. Both are a product of the "hot stove" syndrome. After a little child has touched a hot stove, he or she is doubly reluctant to touch another stove—hot or cold. After enough prospects have been rude, crude, and asinine to you over the phone or in the reception area, you can become pretty "phone shy" and "lobby shy." It is perfectly natural. It would be strange if you didn't feel a reluctance. Pick yourself up, dust yourself off, and start over again from time to time.

There are two ways to deal with the feeling that you just can't pick up the phone to call or walk into the door of a stranger one more time.

The Determination Approach

The determination approach holds that the key to success at the cold call is building a belief system. Belief in yourself, your company, and what you sell. The more belief you have—better stated, the more you believe that what you sell will help others—the easier time you will have making cold calls. There are the four basic beliefs you must own before you can start the cold call process:

- I believe my company is the best.
- I believe my products or services are the best.
- I believe I am the best.
- I believe that when my customers buy from me, they will be better off.

> **KYSO TIP:**
> The real benefit of the cold call is the opportunity to learn to sell and to sell efficiently.

Cold calling will test these beliefs right away. Especially when you begin to get rejected.

The Psychological Approach

The psychological approach works well when there is a lot of stress associated with your call reluctance, particularly the physical kind of stress—sweating, heart racing, and feeling a little shell shocked.

The psychological approach works by knowingly tricking yourself back into the groove. Here are five techniques developed by psychologist Francis Stern. We've seen them work for many call-reluctant salespeople.

Technique 1. Warm up on noncustomers. Work your way up from calls you know will go well to actual cold calls.

- Make your first call to your spouse, best friend, a pal, or a parent. Talk just for a few minutes, five or ten, then move on.
- Make your second call to someone in the company you need to talk to anyway. Again, keep it short.
- Now call someone outside the company who you need to talk to anyway. Your car service person, a travel agent, the laundry that broke all the buttons on your shirt. Again, keep the call brief.
- Need more warm-up? OK. Call a customer. Someone you're already doing business with. Or, you could even make call four to someone you've cold called and succeeded with, and reconfirm the appointment you made on the successful cold call.
- Now, you should be ready! Pick a number, any number, and go for it!

Technique 2. Some salespeople have found that phone calls become easier when they know what each call is worth. Here's how that works. Suppose it takes five phone calls to get one appointment and five appointments to make a $1,000 commission sale. That means that each phone call to a prospect theoretically is worth $40. Simply by logging the number of phone calls you make, you can "track" your daily earnings. The rationale used is simple: "If I am making $40 dollars for every prospect call, whether an appointment results or not, a rejection doesn't hurt as much. I made $40 just for trying."

> **KYSO TIP:**
> The key to cold calling success is to remember to use it, not let it use you. Be in control of the situation and learn, and don't just sell. Cold calling can be the best growth opportunity you have, if you decide to use it.

Technique 3. Some salespeople actually pay themselves for each call. We know one rep who keeps a stack of one-dollar bills in her desk. For each completed call, she puts a single bill in her wallet. She is essentially "earning" her coffee and walking-around money through phone-call making.

Technique 4. Another rep we know occasionally gives his boss's name when talking to a prospect. His logic? Simple. "If I'm feeling a little shell shocked, I start using my boss's name. Then they are rejecting him and not me! The S.O.B could use a little rejection from time to time."

Technique 5. Don't evaluate your phone calls. The task is to call, not to be perfect. After you are back on your feet, you can start working on style and the like. For now, concentrate on calling only.

6

Networking:

Rx for the Cold Call

The cold call may be a great developmental opportunity and, from time to time, a business necessity, especially for beginning salespeople. But it isn't an inevitability or the only route to discovering and meeting new prospects. As any seasoned salesperson can attest, the best prospects are those who walk in the door on their own. People who have seen or heard something about your products or services and want to learn more. But right on the heels of the over-the-transom gift prospect is the networking opportunity, a hot lead developed from out-of-office social, civic, or professional association contacts.

Attending a meeting of a civic, fraternal, charitable, or professional organization almost always has a multitude of agendas for participants—from camaraderie to good works to getting to know potential prospects in a relaxed, convivial atmosphere. Doing a little business along with the work of the organization is expected and accepted as long as you follow the rules.

Helpful Hints for Making the Most of Networking

- *Have a five-year plan.*
- *Make a list of organizations where you can make business contacts and contribute.*
- *Know who the priority contacts are.*
- *Build a thirty-second commercial.*
- *Write down your expected results.*

The Five Basic "Rules" of Networking

1. **Go where the prospects are.** Someone asked famous bank robber Willie Sutton why he robbed banks. *"Cause that's where the money is!"* Willie shot back. Networking that works, first and foremost, means going where your prospects go. It may be Jaycees or Kiwanis, Sertoma, the National Association of Widget Welders, or a service group at your church. It may simply be a one-time meeting or seminar, a positive-thinking rally, or a political caucus.

   NOTE: We are *not* suggesting that every social or civic event you attend, every organization you join or participate in, and every party you go to *must* be used for networking. That is a sure formula for tuning yourself into a social pariah—someone people cross the street to avoid meeting. Business networking may, indeed, be your third or fourth motivation for participation. But, if the opportunity is there, it's foolish not to take advantage of it.

   There are three criteria for evaluating the business networking opportunity of an organization or event.

   - There will be people in attendance who can use your products or services. Jeffrey Gitomer suggests the "50 Butt Rule": If there will be fifty or more butts in the room who are possible prospects, *his* butt will be there as well.
   - You will likely know the names of at least a half dozen people who will be there and whom you could profit from talking to.
   - You have the time to participate fully in the organization or meeting. (No running in for the social hour then ducking out. People observe and recognize *that* behavior for what it is!)

2. **Give first.** Networking follows the Law of Psychological Reciprocity. You have to be willing to give if you are going to get. If you aren't willing to pitch in and participate in the organization's core purpose *and* be a willing business con-

duit for others who are trying to network through the organization, you shouldn't participate. You must be willing to give of yourself. Bread upon the water works!

3. **Dig in.** You must be committed to involvement. Become a person known for contributing time and effort to the mission of the organization or a true civic contributor. Also become known as a person who keeps his or her word on the contact front as well. If you promise to introduce Bob to Jane—do it. If the National Association of Widget Welders is a great group for widget sales leads, you have to be ready, able, and willing to donate to the Widget Welder's Widows Relief Fund, pour punch at the Old Welder's Home, and, in general, get involved in the activities that are important to the association and its members. Sales expert Harvey Mackay is well known in his community—as a civic leader first and a sales expert and author second.[1]

    Besides, if you can't find it in you to whole heartedly support your community and your industry, what sort of dog are you?

4. **Be consistent.** If you've marked out an association or civic group as high potential, attend and attend regularly. You will become known as a doer if you are seen regularly. Jeffrey Gitomer has a one-year wall calendar that lists all the events and meetings he plans on attending and "working." Next to the calendar is a small bulletin board for posting promotional pieces, agendas, and invitations. Every event is rated and ranked for its business potential.

5. **Get to know people.** People tend to do business with people they know and trust—and like. Once they get to know you as a person and as a professional, they will do business with you. Invest the time in getting to know them, and the effort will come back tenfold.

1. Harvey Mackay, *Dig Your Well Before You're Thirsty* (New York: Doubleday Books, 1997).

Working the Room

The actual act of networking can be a lot of fun, if you do it right. Doing it right, of course, means knowing what you're doing. Here are 7.5 steps designed to help you make the most of the social or pre-meeting or pre-program time of any networking event you ever attend.

1. **Target the people you want to meet.** Don't plan on touching base with more than about twenty people. If you spend three minutes with a prospect, that gives you a possibility of twenty people during the social hour (five minutes each for twelve contacts. Double that to ten minutes and your contact list goes down to six people!).

2. **Talk to them.** Talk equals dialogue. Your goal should NOT be to "pitch" everyone you meet. Mostly you want to establish or re-establish yourself in the person's mind. But don't shy away from talking business, either. Soft sell and moderate promotion work best in the more relaxed, social setting.

3. **Establish rapport and find common ground.** Chit chat. Make friends. Figure out what you have in common. Start with some version of the safe, sane, and mundane "Do you come here often?" if you can't find another inroad. Everyone feels a little awkward. Humor can be a nice icebreaker. Just beware; keep the humor light and inoffensive.

4. **Get information that pertains to you from them.** A reasonable goal is to learn one thing about what is going on in the prospect's company you didn't already know, which means letting the other person do most of the talking. Ron Zemke was sans voice for a while a few years ago. Rather than shutting him out, the change from big mouth to big ears branded him "a wonderful conversationalist!"

> **KYSO TIP:**
> At a networking event, almost everyone—well, a lot of people anyway—is there to meet, greet, and possibly sell. You have to wear several hats—seller, buyer, influencer, conduit, etc. Play fair and be willing to wear any or all of those hats as appropriate.

5. **Get them interested in what you do.** Another reasonable goal is to offer a word or two on something you are doing. It could be about something you are doing with a current customer or something new your company is doing (see Chapter 8: The Thirty-Second Commercial).

6. **Write it down.** Summarize every *business* contact on the back of the prospect's business card (or yours if the prospect hasn't one.)

   A. Is the prospect (pick one):

      • In need of your product?
      • Acquainted with someone in need of your product?

- A valuable contact?
- A professional contact?
- A social contact?
- A marginal contact?

B. Qualify the prospect. If the contact is a "need our product" prospect, write a time frame as to when they might need it on the business card *and* this person's leverage over a buying decision.
C. Make an appointment. If there is an immediate need, make an appointment—write it on his or her card and on your card, a card you give to the prospect.

7. **Move on to the next person.** Don't belabor the conversations. Move on when your planned contact time expires. The prospect needs to circulate as well. Watch the prospect's eyes. When they start wandering, so should you. Don't drone on and on about a topic just because you've found one. It's called "Rain Maning"—and no one likes it. Avoid negative, condescending, or gossipy chit chat. You can never be sure if the prospect you're talking to has some connection, interest in, or affiliation with the people, company, or product you're slamming.

7.5. **Follow up.** Whether you've made a commitment for a meeting or simply promised to share some information, follow up within the next twenty-four hours. Responsiveness counts.

Networking vs. Stalking the PTA

The secret to networking is being in the right places—at the right time. By and large, buttonholing people and trying to whip up business at the grade school open house or parents' night is a little pushier than most of us care to be. And it runs the risk of turning you into the aforementioned social pariah. But a few well-chosen words at a social gathering is another matter.

For example: You are at the neighborhood barbecue. Everyone is there including Bob and Jane, who just moved into the

Smith place down on the cul de sac. Someone introduces you. You learn that Bob is with Multiworld Systems, a company you've been trying to get into for two years.

It's not going to fracture the fabric of space and time or cause Bob and Jane to double deadbolt their doors if you simply say: "Bob, I've been calling on your company for a couple of years. Maybe one day you could give me some tips on how to get a hearing in your place." Leave it at that, and nobody goes away feeling violated or the occasion debased.

Net-Net

Networking is simple. Networking is powerful. Networking makes selling—and the selling process—easier and more enjoyable.

Networking is not an optional before or after business hour activity. Networking is a vital and integral part of your sales success.

FACT: The most powerful business relationships are not built during business hours.

> **KYSO TIP:**
> Knock Your Socks Off salespeople *do* business between 9 and 5, and *build* business before and after "regular" business hours.

How do you integrate networking into your business schedule? Ten hours a month of intelligent, selective networking can have a doubling effect on your business growth—and in just a few months.

7

The Referral:

Handle with Care

The gold standard of leads is the referral. It is the second most coveted prize in selling—right after the sale. It is a symbol of trust on the part of a customer and a sign of respect to be treated with care.

Ask...Politely

Here's the straight. A good customer, someone you've been doing business with, who you like and who seems to like you, someone you can kid with, talk hobbies and life conundrums with, would be insulted if you didn't ask for a **referral**—an introduction to a friend or associate who might have a need for your product or service. Even customers with whom you have a more formal relationship will respond positively to a request for an introduction.

There are two types of referral requests: the **specific prospect introduction** and the **broad request**.

The Specific Prospect Introduction

"Stan, I believe you mentioned that you know Mark Sparks at Acme Industries. Could I impose on you to introduce us?"

"Mary, I'm trying to meet Joe at Silver Meadow Printing. Could you introduce us?"

The Broad Request

"Stan, I know you've been pleased with our services. Do you know other Widget Picklers who might have a use for our services?"

"Mary, I know you've been pleased with the work we've done for you. Are there others you know who could profit from our services?"

The hard part is what you do with the referral once your customer honors you with it. Here are ten tips for making the most of a referral.

Tip One. Approach with care, be prepared, don't move too quickly. Timing is everything. Don't appear too anxious—to either the referrer or the referee. A proper set-up will breed a long-term relationship. Don't be aggressive with your client. You want him or her to see the referral as a gift from him or her to you, not an uncomfortable obligation. Don't be overly aggressive with the referee. Demanding an appointment because Stan or Mary referred you makes Stan and Mary look bad to their acquaintance.

Tip Two. Arrange a three-way meeting. The ideal approach to a referral is arm and arm with your customer, a three-way, face-to-face meeting.

- Arrange for the three of you to meet at a social, fraternal, or association event.
- Arrange a meal—breakfast or lunch is more business-like. Dinners are more casual.
- Arrange to meet at a networking event.
- Have your customer accompany you to a prearranged meeting on the prospect's premises.

If none of those are possible or practical, try to:

- Arrange a phone call to the referral from your customer telling of your impending call.
- Arrange for your referral to write a letter of introduction.

These approaches, by and far, are the premium of referrals. They put you in front of a prospect with someone else singing your praises. A third-party referral and endorsement are more powerful than a hundred cold call presentations.

Tip Three. Get personal information about the referral before you make the first contact. Business information, personal information, recent successes, likes, last vacation, children's schools, hometown, and the like. Having personal information is an advantage. Not having personal information is a fatal mistake. You need to know more about a referral prospect than name, rank, and serial number. Your customer can give you the facts of his or her relationship—that's step one. Step two is to gather information from other sources. What info do you need? In *Swim with the Sharks*,[1] Harvey Mackay tells us that salespeople in his company gather 66 pieces of information on customers and prospects—from their birth date to the children's names to their religious affiliation. The point isn't to become a voyeur, but to know enough about the prospect to create a friendly, nondefensive atmosphere so your product or service gets a free hearing.

Tip Four. You don't have to sell at the first meeting if your customer is with you. In fact, the less selling you do, the more credible you will appear. You only have to establish rapport, gain confidence, and pave the way to...

Tip Five. Arrange a second, private meeting. There, you can get down to business and talk about his needs, your company, and your products and services.

Tip Six. Try to get the prospect to prepare information for your meeting. If you can get the prospect to gather and/or compile information, you have an interested prospect who will be willing to talk and listen. OK. This can be a stretch, but here's where you are. (1) You already know there's a sales potential here; (2) you've been introduced and vouched for as a good reli-

1. Harvey Mackay. *Swim with the Sharks* (New York: Ballantine, 1997).

able person to do business with; and (3) you've said "hello" and asked for a chance to talk business. You might say something like, "Bill, when we meet on the 18th I'd like an opportunity to review your current Widget usage and costs to see if there is a way I can (save you some money/help you with the reject problem/show you some alternatives)." Let the prospect know you're willing to get down to business and lend a helping hand. He'll appreciate the focus.

Tip Seven. Don't send too much information in the mail. (You won't make a sale in the mail.) The mail, like the phone, is not where a sale is made. It's just a sales tool. Send just enough to inform and create interest.

Tip Eight. Write a personal note to the referral within twenty-four hours. Be brief, but positive. Don't weigh the note down with superfluous thinks. Just tell him or her it was nice to get acquainted and you're looking forward to the next meeting.

Tip Nine. Write your customer a note of thanks. Include a gift if the sale will be of some significance (a quality ad specialty—something with your logo printed on it, or two tickets to a ball game.) If you give a gift, make it memorable. Send something that will be talked about. Your thanks and gift will encourage the customer to get you another referral.

NOTE: Be sure of the company's gift policy before blundering into an embarrassing situation.

Tip Ten. Deliver! Failure to follow up and deliver as promised makes you and your customer look bad to the prospect. Failure to deliver also eliminates any chance of another referral. This rule is the most important of them all; it is a breeding ground for your reputation.

Least Preferred Referred

One final "real world" note. The least preferred or productive way to use a referral, but the way it seems to happen most often, is in a cold call (or letter) to a name, address, and number given to you by a customer or friend. Be creative. Make it a meaningful and personal connection. Get some information about the referral and his or her company before the first contact is made. Don't fall into the trap of calling or writing and saying, "I was given your name by ...." That sounds horrible.

> **KYSO TIP:**
> "When you get a referral, treat it like gold. One third-party endorsement is worth a hundred presentations...if you know what you're doing."
>
> **Anonymous**

Say instead:

> *"Hi, my name is Jeffrey Gitomer, my company is Business Marketing Services, and you don't know me from a sack of potatoes. I've been doing business with (name of customer) for some time now, and she thought I might be able to help you in the same way I've helped her."*

Do some rapport building.

> *"I'm told you're quite a ... ... ,"* or *"I heard your business just...."*

Move out before your welcome is worn out.

> *"I just wanted to touch base, introduce myself, and get your address to send you some information I think you'll find to be of interest."*

If the chat is going well, you might say something else to establish personal rapport before you sign off. Perhaps you can get the referral to laugh. Then say, "I'll call you back in a few days, and maybe we can find a time to talk over lunch. Thanks for your time."

Don't be too windy. You're not going to make the sale on the phone. Say just enough to whet the appetite.

8

The Thirty-Second Commercial:

Key to Memorable Contacts

There are dozens of business occasions every week—if not every day—when it would be just great to have a little personal commercial in your pocket; a little statement of who you are, what you do, and why someone would want you to do it for them. Don't believe it? How many trade shows, business meetings, and networking events have you been to where you've had a rapid-fire spate of three- to five-minute contacts—and come away with no idea of how many of those suspects—potential prospects—will even remember having shaken your hand and saying "Howdy?"

With a well-written, polished personal commercial, you can take the ambiguity out of your mind—you will be remembered.

Let's say you're out with a customer networking at her trade association meeting, and she introduces you to a prospect. The prospect says, "What do you do?" If you're in the temporary staffing industry and you say, "I'm in the temporary staffing industry," you have just blown a gold-plated opportunity! Your reply should have been, "We provide quality emergency and temporary employees for businesses like yours so that when one of your own employees is sick, absent, or on vacation, there is no loss of productivity or reduction of service to your customers." You deliver a line like *that* and the prospect can't help but be impressed. He knows what your business is, and that you are a pro.

Now you have the prospect's attention. You can even—should even—move on and ask a question or two to find out how qualified the prospect is. "How many employees do you have?" you might ask. "Do you give them one or two weeks vacation?" "How do you ensure that the level of service to your customers isn't reduced during these vacation times?" Make the prospect think a little.

Building the Thirty-Second Commercial

Your objective is to have thirty seconds of information that

- States who you are,
- Who your company is,
- Creatively tells what you do (in terms of the prospect),
- Asks one or a series of Power Questions,
- Makes a Power Statement that shows how you can help others, and
- Ends with why the prospect should act now. A call to action.

Let's unwrap that list a little. After you creatively say what you do, you ask a Power Question or series of questions that prompts the prospect to think and respond in a way that gives you added information about him and his company or his personal situation.

This information lets you know how qualified the prospect may be and allows you to formulate an impact response to show how you can help. The questions should be open ended. A question that gets the prospect thinking and talking, not just saying yes or no.

NOTE: There is no real reason to tell a prospect how you can help until you have uncovered what kind of help he or she needs.

The Power Question is the most critical part of the process because it qualifies the prospect and sets up your high-impact response. When formulating the Power Questions for your commercial, ask yourself these five questions:

1. What information do I want to get as a result of asking this question?
2. Can I qualify my prospect as a result of the question?
3. Does it take more than one question to find out the information I need?
4. Do my questions make the prospect think?
5. Can I ask a question that separates me from my competitors?

NOTE: Chapter 10 goes into more detail on Power Questions and Power Statements, but this checklist and the following example should get you started.

Here is an example of a personal commercial.

Name:

"Hi, my name is Richard Herd."

Company name:

"I'm the president of Continental Advertising."

Creatively say what you do:

"We impact your image, create sales, and ensure repeat business by providing innovative advertising specialties that keep your name in front of your customers and prospects."

Insert your Power Question:

"How are you currently using ad specialties? (variations— What are you doing to keep your name in front of your customers every day? How often do you contact your present customers? What are you doing to ensure your name is in front of your customers more than your competitors?)"

Insert your Power Statement (how you help):

"I think we can help you. We have creative brainstorming sessions with our clients where we bring together a small team of our people and yours. We place various items on the table that relate to your business and the customers you

serve. This process creates dialog that always leads to innovative products that complement your marketing plan and impact your customer's image of you. Not only is it productive, it's fun."

NOTE: A preplanned Power Statement is very important, but be sensitive to the answer to your Power Question. It may dictate you go in a wholly different direction than you preplanned.

Why the Prospect Should Act Now

"Would you like to schedule a lunch and preview a few items to get a better feel for what I mean?"

> *Use this example to help you write your own commercial. After you write it, rehearse it. Then try it out and adjust it for the real world. Then really practice it (in more than twenty-five times in real situations) until you own it.*

Your Personal Commercial Worksheet

Name _____

Company Name _____

What You Do (briefly) _____

_____

_____

Power Question _____

_____

_____

Power Statement _____

_____

_____

How You Help _____

_____

_____

Why People Should Contact You Now _____

_____

_____

Instructions: Fill out the form, read it from top to bottom, add a few personal pronouns, time it, practice it, and voilà!

9

Cultivating Top Down Sales

Question: What do the Solomon R. Guggenheim Museum of Art in New York City and Knock Your Socks Off Selling have in common?

Answer: Both are more enjoyable if you start at the top.

How's That?

The Guggenheim Museum, designed by Frank Lloyd Wright, is a ten-story, inverted cone of a building, open through its center, with a sweeping top-to-bottom spiral ramp gallery. Visitors are encouraged to ride the elevator to the topmost level of the museum and take in the displays of modern and contemporary art as they stroll casually back down to ground level.

Knock Your Socks Off Selling goes more smoothly the further up the client organization you start. How far up? As far up as you dare. Rule of thumb: The further up the organization you can start, the more success you are likely to meet. OK. OK. There is also a rule of reasonableness here as well. If you are selling maintenance services or copy paper or security services, you possibly don't want to be making a cold call on the chairman of a Fortune 500 company. Then again, in a medium or small company, it may be perfectly reasonable to set your sights at the very top. For whatever you sell.

The power of being introduced to the actual decision maker by the CEO is better than a Christmas when Santa brings you everything on your list.

Getting to the CEO can be tricky. If you just ask for the president, the owner, the boss, or the fearless leader, you *may* get through, but it will pay off better if you to prepare a bit before you start making cold calls to the CEO, especially if the prospect you are targeting represents an important sale to you.

Here is a four-step plan for contacting and scoring a CEO appointment:

1. **Get ready before you start. You only have one shot at it, make it your best one.**

   - Have a written game plan. Target one to ten companies and define in writing what you want to accomplish by calling on the CEO and what it will take to get what you want.
   - Be totally prepared to sell before you make the call. Have everything (sales pitch, thirty-second commercial, concept explanation, samples, daily planner) prepared and in front of you before you make the first call.
   - Identify the leader (by name) and get as much information and as many characteristics as you can. Make preliminary calls to the CEO's underlings, associates of yours who might know the company and the CEO, and associations the CEO might be a part of to get pertinent information before you make the big call.

EXAMPLE: We both frequently receive telephone cold calls at our offices. It is amazing how many people call and ask to speak with Ronald Zemeck instead of Ron Zemke and Jeff Gittiler instead of Jeffrey Gitomer. There is absolutely no way anyone is going to get through to talk to either of us if he or she can't pronounce our names correctly—it just won't happen. And rightly so. If the prospect is important enough to call on, he's important enough to accurately identify. Get the basic facts correct before making your call.

2. Use the right tactics when getting to and getting through...

- ASK FOR HELP with your homework. Buttonhole any-one you know who might know the CEO you are going to call on, or who knows someone who knows the CEO.
- When you approach the president's secretary, it's help-ful to have his secretary's or personal assistant's name. If you don't, listen carefully—or ask for it—and use it during the call.
- Be polite, but firm.
- Be professional.
- Persist. You can't take the first no or rebuff as a final decision. Ac-knowledge the gate-keeper's or influ-encer's reluctance to give you information and add something like, "I'm just trying to make sure that I'm prepared when we fi-nally talk."

> **EXAMPLE:**
> *You call and the secretary says,*
> *Sally: Mr. Jones is on vacation.*
> *You: Wow, that's great, Sally. Where did he go?*
> *While you are chatting Sally up, listen for anything personal you can (golf, sales meeting time, staff meeting time, impor-tant new product) and refer to it subtly when you get him or her on the phone.*

- It's risky to call for the CEO without having his or her name. A fallback is to try, "How do you spell his last name?" but it's embarrassing to hear "J-O-N-E-S."
- If the gatekeeper won't put you through the first time...

  ❖ Ask for the CEO's extension or direct-dial number from the secretary or assistant. If he or she says no, you can always call back and ask the switchboard person.
  ❖ Inquire as to the best time to call. Some senior peo-ple do have vendor call hours.
  ❖ Find out when he or she usually arrives.
  ❖ Find out when he or she takes lunch.

❖ Find out who sets his or her calendar.

❖ Find out if he or she leaves the building at lunch or eats at the desk.

❖ Find out when he or she leaves for the day.

• Make sure the person closest to the boss likes you.

• If you are a risk taker, take a chance on humor. Try this line on Sally or Sam: "I know you actually run the company, but could I speak to the person who thinks they do?"

> **KYSO TIP:**
> Some CEOs like to be in the office an hour or two before the daily hubbub begins—others like staying late to close out the day. Some like to use Saturday mornings for catch-up and think time. Without someone in the gatekeeper's seat, the likelihood of your call going through goes up. Without good rapport with the assistant or secretary, you'll never know this vital tidbit.

What you are looking for is any information that can increase the probability that a call from you to the CEO (or the senior-most person you think will give you good leverage) will get through and get you a positive—not just polite—hearing.

3. When you get him or her on the phone, move quickly.

• Have your opening line ready and rehearsed.

• Get right to the point. Avoid chitchat and relationship-building rhetoric—there won't be time.

• Make your message compelling (have the best Power Question and Power Statement of your life at hand).

• If you are asking for a face-to-face appointment (and not just an inside referral), ask for no more than five minutes (offer to be thrown out if your visit goes past five minutes).

• Have five comebacks or counters ready to go in the event you are initially rebuffed. The first one should start with "I understand…."

Notes About the CEO and the Process...

- CEOs are hard to get to, harder to appoint, and easiest to sell.
- If the CEO is interested in your product or service, he or she will take you by the hand and introduce you to the team member who can actually do the deal.
- The CEO always knows where to send you to get the job done.
- If the CEO tries to send you to someone else without a hearing, it means you have not delivered a powerful enough message and he's not interested. The solution? Fix it. Keep trying until you get an appointment.
- If you start lower than the top, there is risk. No matter how powerful someone *not* the CEO says he or she is or appears to be, he or she usually has to ask someone else for final approval. Not so for CEOs. They usually just ask their secretary or administrative assistant if they liked you. Get the picture?

The Benefits Are Obvious

- The leader is always the decider, or has the option to be the final arbiter.
- The CEO may not be directly involved in purchasing what you're selling, but his or her introduction after a brief "interest-generating" meeting can be the difference between a full and attentive hearing, and the difference between a sale and no sale.
- The power of being introduced to the decision maker by the CEO is as real as you would hope it is.

Beware of the Hand-Off

If the boss tries to hand you off too early (before the proposed five-minute meeting), don't accept it. Say "I appreciate your wanting to delegate, but the reason I wanted to meet with you personally is that this will impact your business significantly. I'd like five minutes to show you the highlights and get your reaction before I talk with anyone else in your firm. I know your time is valuable. If I take more than five minutes, you can throw me out."

4. Make your five-minute meeting the best you ever had.

- Have a proposal in writing. One page only.
- Have notes on everything you want to cover.
- Have a list of anticipated questions and answers.
- Have samples or something to demonstrate.
- Have credibility builders—your best testimonial letter, something in print.
- Practice your presentation—aloud.
- Be early.
- Look as sharp as you've ever looked.
- Be knowledgeable. Have answers in terms of how your product or service works for the buyer.

- Be memorable. The thing that sets you apart, the thing that gets remembered, is the thing that leads to the sale.
- Deliver. You have one chance. Don't blow it by not following through.

The Secret of Top Down Selling Is the 4.5 Rs...

- Be resourceful. Look for a route to the top person others have missed.
- Be ready (prepared). Rule of thumb: forty hours of homework for a five-minute CEO interview.
- Be relentless. Keep trying regardless of the number and nature of the rebuffs.
- Be remembered. Distinguish yourself—positively.
- There is a 4.5 "R"—risk it.

The gift shop at the Guggenheim has a T-shirt that says "Start at the Top." How much more of a wake-up call do you need? Call them and order one today (www.guggenheim.org or 212-423-3555).

> *It's the most challenging, rewarding fun you can have in sales!*

10

Questions, Questions, Questions:

Keys to Understanding

Somehow a lot of salespeople have come to believe that selling is talking; making a grand, convincing argument that the prospect can't resist. Knock Your Socks Off Selling is, first and foremost, about listening. Understanding what a prospect needs and wants. What a prospect is reluctant or fearful about. How the prospect thinks and evaluates. What will make the prospect look and feel smart, capable, and confident. Knock Your

> *"It is better to know some of the questions, rather than all of the answers."*
>
> *James Thurber*

Socks Off Selling is about gathering and using information to make a match between a prospect's wants and needs and your products and services. Knock Your Socks Off Selling is, first and foremost, about asking good questions and getting useful answers.

Sure, you make presentations and explain your products and services to prospects, but the basis of the best presentation is the information you've gathered on, and from, the prospect via skillful, careful—and most of all—thoughtful questioning.

Asking the right questions helps you:

- Qualify the buyer.
- Build credibility.
- Establish rapport.
- Identify needs.

72

- Find hot buttons.
- Gauge progress.
- Create buying tension.

- Understand the situation.
- Check for understanding.
- Close the sale.

It just takes asking the right questions at the right time.

Open and Closed Questions

There are two general types of questions—open and closed. It is vital to know the difference and when and how to use each.

Closed Questions are answered with a yes or no. They are used to establish facts or specific pieces of information, confirm agreement, focus the conversation, or limit options.

- "You are currently using Wexley Widgets, aren't you Mr. Smith?"
- "Your primary concern is with widget quality and reliability, isn't it Mr. Smith?"
- "If we could guarantee an uninterrupted flow of two to twelve titanium widgets for seventy-two weeks, that would meet your needs?"

Open-Ended Questions promote dialog and conversation, encourage exploration, elicit feelings, generate options, and engage and involve the prospect. Good open-ended questions help the prospect think through his or her situation and evaluate his or her options.

> **KYSO TIP:**
> A study comparing high- and average-performing salespeople found that high-performing salespeople asked 60 percent more open-ended and 17 percent fewer closed questions than average-performing salespeople.

- "What are the strengths and weaknesses of your current suppliers?"
- "If you were designing the perfect widget from the ground up, what would it look like?"
- "How is your widget inventory managed right now?"

Probing Questions are a special subset of open-ended questions. Probing questions help you delve more deeply into a prospect's needs, problems, and complaints and move in the direction of creating solutions for him and opportunities for you.

To move toward developing a proposal, a hotel banquet manager might ask:

- "Can you tell me more about your event—who will be attending, what will they be expecting, and how could we improve on last year's event?"

A retailer might approach a browsing customer and simply ask:

- "What features are you looking for in an off-road bike?"

Probing questions are a way for you to gather information. If the answer the prospect gives sounds impossible—untrue, off the wall, a stretch of the imagination—don't argue; just ask another probing question.

A good source for creating probing questions are the five Ws: who, what, when, where, and why. You can toss in the occasional "how" for variety.

- "Who is affected by this?"
- "What would you like to see in a phone system?"
- "When do you need the new system in place?"
- "Where will the new assembly line be?"
- "Can you tell me why you need such a high tensile strength?"
- "How do you warehouse part blanks now?"

The exact questions you need to ask will vary from situation to situation and from prospect to prospect. When in doubt—or simply when you aren't sure of what the prospect just told you— you can almost always fall back on the tried and true, all-purpose probing question: "Can you tell me more about that?"

Confirming Questions make sure that you aren't assuming too much and *confirm* what you think you know. They also give the prospect an opportunity to add information or clarify what has been discussed.

- "So, if we can ship you a partial order tomorrow, you would be good through the weekend and we could set up a regular supply schedule on Monday, right?"
- "Let me make sure I have this. You are looking for a better-quality widget than you are buying now, but you need to keep the cost below premium, is that right?"

Power Questions

So far we've been talking about questions that will garner and confirm valuable information about the prospect, the situation, and his or her organization. An important job. But there is another kind of question that serves another purpose—or at least an added purpose. This is the **Power Question**—a question designed to make the prospect or customer stop and say, "No one ever asked me that before!" Power Questions cause the prospect to stop and think before responding, to look at the problem or need or opportunity in a new way. Power Questions distinguish you from the competition and establish a buying, rather than a selling, atmosphere. Power Questions give the prospect a new and different perspective and—sometimes—a different motivation for buying than he started out with. Power Questions tell the prospect that *you* are the kind of person he needs to talk with often.

Power Questions, to be Power Questions, should do one or more of the following:

- Be clear and concise—easy to understand.
- Require productive thinking on the prospect's part.
- Encourage the prospect to share past experience
- Prod the prospect to evaluate new information or ideas.
- Lead the prospect to a new response or idea.
- Relate directly to the prospect's objectives.
- Draw out information that makes the sale easier.
- Create a positive atmosphere and be conducive to selling.

Power Questions aren't easy to come by or create—or everyone would use them. When you find one, hang on to it and use it carefully and well. There is no magic formula, save challenging yourself to think about the prospect's needs in a different way than the prospect—or the competition—is thinking about it. Examples help.

Mundane Question	Power Version
• Do you have a pager?	• If your most important client called you right now, how would you get the message?
• Who is your long-distance carrier?	• If your long-distance rates were 30 percent higher than they should be, how would you know?
• What type of life insurance do you have?	• If you died tomorrow, how would your children go to college?

Notice two things about these questions. All three make the prospect think in terms of his or her own interests, and all three imply that the asker has some special insight into what would constitute a good answer.

EXAMPLE: In a recent workshop Jeffrey Gitomer was conducting, Scott Wells, a Time Warner Cable TV salesperson from Raleigh, North Carolina, was looking for a power question that would help him qualify prospects and get them thinking about premium channels. With a little urging he came up with:

"If you owned your own cable channel, Mrs. Jones, what would be on it?"

It is a question that draws out the likes and dislikes of the prospect and frames the answer in terms of an assumed sale:

"Well, I would have _____ , _____ , and _____ on my cable station."

The **stem**, or front part or lead-in of a question, is often the hardest part to generate on your own. Below are twenty Power Question stems that will help you quickly uncover a prospect's area of need.

• What do you look for...?	• What have you found...?
• How do you propose...?	• What has been your experience...?
• How have you successfully used...?	• How do you determine...?
• Why is that a deciding factor...?	• What makes you choose...?
• What do you like about...?	• What is one thing you would improve about...?
• What would you change about...?	• Are there other factors...?
• What does your competitor do about...?	• How do your customers react to...?
• How are you currently...?	• What are you doing to keep...?
• How often do you contact...?	• What are you doing to ensure...?
• How do you evaluate...?	• What do you think is...?

Jeffrey created the following eight Power Questions to help him help prospects for sales training think about sales training in a different way:

1. "How many of your salespeople missed their sales goals last year?"
2. "What was the major cause?"

3. "What plans have you made to ensure they will meet them this year?"
4. "What sort of personal development plans do you ask your people to set?"
5. "How do you support their sales efforts?"
6. "How much did you budget for sales training last year?"
7. "How much do you wish you had budgeted?"
8. "When training takes place, how do you track each individual's progress?"

These questions ask Jeffrey's prospects to think about sales training in a different light and to consider what Jeffrey has to offer as well.

Sequencing and Setting Up Power Questions

Except when you are giving your thirty-second commercial, Power Questions need to be set up to be most effective. That's what all the other types of questions are for. A nice model for pacing your delivery is sales consultant Ray Leone's three-stage strategy for setting up and asking questions.

First stage: Make a factual statement that can't be refuted.

Second stage: Make a personal observation that reflects your experience and creates credibility.

Third stage: Ask an open-ended question that incorporates the first two stages.

Let's say you are selling copiers.

First stage:

- "You know, Mr. Jones, document processing is an integral part of the operation of any business."

Second stage:

- "My experience has shown me that many businesses fail to put enough emphasis on the quality and cost control of their documents. They fail to realize that every time a copy is sent to a customer, it reflects the image and quality of your business."

(Now it's time for you to drop the question.)

Third stage:

- "How are you ensuring that the quality of your copies reflects the quality of your business?"

As an owner of a business, that question would make me think. One more. Let's say you are an accountant.

First stage:

- "You know, Mr. Jones, most businesses don't plan long enough in advance for their best tax advantage."

Second stage:

- "My experience has shown me that entrepreneurs lack the financial expertise to do their own planning and then blame it on a lack of time. That's what led us to put together this tax planner. It takes about an hour a month, is simple to use, and can save you thousands of dollars every year."

Third stage:

- "How are you planning for your taxes for 1999? With your permission, I'd like to review your 1998 return and customize your planner for the type of financial situations you face day to day. I'm sure you're looking to save every tax penny you can and want an accountant who will fight the IRS to keep every dollar allowed under the law, don't you?"

How can you say no to that? You can't!

When Questions Go Wrong

The right question, poorly timed or badly worded, can undo all of the good will and selling magic you've worked so hard to create. When questions go wrong, typically one of four things has happened:

1. **The question was asked at the wrong time, possibly out of sequence.** There is a logic to the order in which questions should be asked. For example, it's generally easy to verify a prospect's name early in the conversation, and often very awkward to do so after the two of you finish a thirty-minute conversation.

   - *"Jeff, is McLeod M-C or M-A-C? I know it could be spelled several ways. I keep people's names in an electronic database, so spelling is important."*

2. **The prospect thought you were asking about something you already know,** or that he or she believes you should know.i Use the *preview* technique to explain why you need to ask.

   - *"Mr. Ruiz, I know that Gee Whiz is a big user of Widgets. And I've seen some of your literature, but could you give me the two-minute drill version of your positioning in the industry?"*

3. **The prospect feels you are asking too many questions.** Make your questions count, for you and for your prospect. Power Questions are never seen as trivial if they are thought out and information based. Prospects

can smell out a "fishing expedition" in a minute. Better to discuss the weather than unleash a strong of trivial questions. If you are sitting in a prospect's office and don't already know he is a widget user, why are you there?

4. **The question feels too personal.** What's personal and what's just conversation will vary from person to person. If you're asking because you're curious, it may be better not to. If you're asking because you need the information, use the preview technique to explain why before you ask.

- *"In order for us to build the best financial plan for you, I'll need to ask you some important questions about your personal finances. Of course, all the information we work with today will remain confidential. Do you have any questions before we begin?"*

Build a Catalog

You can't have too many examples of Power Questions. Make a Power Question file. Every time you hear a good one—write it down! Even if it's coming from a prospect or someone who is prospecting you. Just stop and say, "Oh wow! What a great question! Let me write that down. I don't want to forget it!" They'll be flattered and amused.

> *"Only when you begin to ask the right question do you begin to find the right answers."*
>
> Dorothy Leeds

Go back to the Power Questions earlier in this chapter and the ones in Chapter 8, The Thirty-Second Commercial, write them out in your words, and put them in your Power Question file. Another super source for learning more about question building and using are two books by Dorothy Leeds, an internationally known business, sales, and communication consultant.

They are: *Smart Questions: A New Strategy for Successful Managers* (Berkley, 1995) and *PowerSpeak* (Berkley, 1996).

Power Statements—The Other Shoe

Power Statements are the follow-up to a great sequence of information gathering, stage setting, and Power Questioning. They are also vital memory pegs for your thirty-second commercial and ear-catching assertions for your prospect presentation.

What is a Power Statement? A statement that makes your product or service outstanding, understandable, credible (incredible), and buyable. A nontraditional or unusual statement that describes what you do and how you do it in terms of the customer and his or her perceived use or need of what you're selling.

Here are three Power Statements that answer the question, "So what do you do?" in an eye-popping memorable way:

1. **Temporary accounting help:**

   "We provide quality emergency and temporary accounting staff for businesses like yours so that when one of your own is sick, absent, or on vacation, there is no loss of productivity or reduction of vigilance or service to your customers."

2. **Men's clothing:**

   "Our experience has shown us that salespeople dress for their customers. We create the look you need to make that important presentation."

3. **A variation:**

   "When our customers have an important meeting or speech to make, they go to their closet and select clothing they bought from us."

These Power Statements creatively say what the speaker does in terms of the prospect's needs.

Power Statements Also Can Be Memorable Opening Lines

Jeffrey likes to tell the following story:

> *"I went to one of those business opportunity [franchise] shows. Companies trying to sell businesses for $10,000 to $150,000. There were more than 100 businesses represented. Half were immediately recognizable by their national stature.*
>
> *I took my tape recorder because I was sure I would hear dozens of gems. What I heard was disappointing (pathetic). After the first twenty or so duds, I was hoping to find just one. I did. As I walked by a booth loaded with Mickey Mouse products and clothing, a woman met me in the aisle and said, Mickey Mouse makes more money in a year than every company in this room...combined! What a line. I thanked her for making my day—she gave me a puzzled, You're welcome."*

Power Statements Generate Interest and Get Appointments

Generic-Interest Power Statement: "Your key to profits is productivity. Last year we grew sales by more than 300 percent by providing items that arrived on time and aided our customers' productivity. In 30 days we can improve yours."

Generic-Appointment Power Statement: "I'm not sure if I can help you, Mr. Johnson. Let me explore some details with you for a few minutes (or over lunch). If I think I can help you, I'll tell you, and if I can't, I'll tell you that, too. Fair enough?"

Creating Your Own Power Statements

Creating Power Statements is just that, a creative, think-sideways process. Here's the mind-set:

- Don't sell drill bits, sell the smooth perfect holes they create.
- Don't sell printing, sell the brochures that will reflect your prospect's image and impact her sales.
- Don't sell cars, sell the prestige and status the prospect will have, or the smooth ride.
- Don't sell insurance, sell safe, financially secure families protected from tragedy.
- Don't sell eyeglasses, sell better vision and stylish looks.

How do you know one when you've written one? Here are twelve criteria to test your efforts against.

1. A statement that makes a prospect think about what you do in terms of how he or she can use what you offer.
2. A statement that builds your credibility with a prospect.
3. A nontraditional statement that describes what you do and how you do it in terms of benefits to your prospect.
4. A statement about what you do in terms of what your prospect needs.

5. A statement that draws a clear line of distinction between you and your competitor.
6. A statement that makes the prospect want to hear more.
7. A statement that gives the customer a reason to buy.
8. A statement that breaks down resistance.
9. A statement that gives the customer more confidence to buy.
10. A statement that makes a favorable impact on the prospect.
11. A statement that links what you do and how it relates to the prospect.
12. A statement that is memorable.

THE BEST TEST of all—corner a friend, your spouse, a coworker, or a forgiving customer, read them your five best Power Statements, and watch their reactions. The ones that light their eyes and garner a WOW are the keepers.

11

Anticipating Customer Needs and Expectations:

The Rater Factors

Customers and prospects are demanding. And they have every right to be. Today's customers have more options than ever before. If your organization doesn't offer what they want or need, if you don't interact with them in a manner that meets or exceeds their expectations, they will just walk down the street—or let their fingers walk through the Yellow Pages—and do business with one of your competitors.

That's why companies spend a lot of time and money observing customers as they shop, surveying them by mail, talking to them on the phone, and meeting them face to face. Like miners working a claim for the gold they know is there, today's businesses collect and sort customer intelligence, looking for clues about what people want and why they buy today—and how their needs may change tomorrow.

As a sales professional, you draw on the knowledge your company has acquired about customers. But you have another, equally important source of information: your own day-to-day contact with your customers. From personal experience, you know quite a lot about what your customers want—and what disappoints them. That's your own special edge, the foundation on which to build your own unique way of creating Knock Your Socks Off Sales.

Getting Yourself Organized

It's helpful to have a framework to hold together the things you know personally, the information passed on to you by your organization, and what you learn by asking questions and by listening to your customers. One framework we like a lot was invented by Texas A&M researcher Dr. Leonard Berry. He and his colleagues observe that customers evaluate the companies and people they do business with on five dimensions or factors:

> *"Customer expectations of organizations are loud and clear: look good, be responsive, be reassuring through courtesy and competence, be empathetic, but, most of all, be reliable. Do what you said you would do. Keep your promises."*
>
> *Dr. Leonard Berry*
> *Researcher, Texas A&M*
> *University*

1. **Reliability.** The ability to provide what was promised, dependably and accurately.
2. **Assurance.** The knowledge and courtesy you show to customers, and your ability to convey trust, competence, and confidence.
3. **Tangibles.** The physical facilities and equipment of your organization, its marketing materials, and your appearance.
4. **Empathy.** The degree of caring and individual attention you show customers.
5. **Responsiveness.** Your willingness to respond in a timely manner and help customers promptly when asked.

Chances are, almost everything you do to and for your customers falls into one of these categories. Consider these common examples:

1. When you provide a prospect with information he or she requested, you show *reliability*.
2. When you smile and tell a customer, "I can show you an easy way to finance that"—and do—you build *assurance; confidence in your expertise*.

3. When you take the time to make yourself presentable and your presentation materials tailored and first class, you are paying attention to the *tangibles*.

4. When you are sensitive to a customer's specific needs during a presentation, you show *empathy*.

5. When your prospect asks you to provide two more product packages—ASAP—and you deliver within the hour, you show *responsiveness*.

> **KYSO TIP:**
> These five universal customer expectations can be your secret weapon for creating Power Questions that get your prospect's attention and for building presentations that focus on his or her most important hot buttons. Watch for them—and note them carefully—in everything your prospect reveals to you.

All five factors are critically important to winning your customer's confidence and business. Let's look more closely at each of them to see how they combine to create prospect-pleasing Knock Your Socks Off Sales.

Reliability

Reliability means doing to and for the customer what you say you will do. To the customer, there are *three distinct promises* that are important.

- **Organizational commitments.** Organizations make direct promises to customers through advertising and marketing materials, in company correspondence and contracts, and in service guarantees and policies published for everyone to see. In addition to these, customers will hold the company to indirect commitments—promises that customers believe are implied in the way the company talks about itself, its products, and its services. Your job is to show the prospect—prove to her—how your organization will keep all the stated and implied commitments.

- **Common expectations.** Your customers bring additional expectations with them to every relationship. Based on their past experiences with you and with other vendors, customers make assumptions about what you can and can't do for them. Failing to meet a customer expectation, whether or not you knew about it, has the same impact as breaking any other promise. Your task is to uncover all your customer's expectations. Any time a prospect answers a question about quality delivery or performance expectations with, "Oh, you know, the usual," common expectations are at work. Probe them. Ferret them out. "Mr. Smith, we pride ourselves on being a cut above the usual company. Can we go over some specifics?"
- **Personal promises.** The majority of promises come from you. These are the promises you make when you tell a customer, "I'll get right back to you with that information," or "I'll deliver that contract in two days," or "I understand the problem you are having with your computer, and our software will solve it."

Knowing what your customers expect is the first step to Knock Your Socks Off Selling. By asking questions and really listening, you'll be able to discover the details of the implied promise your customers expect you to fulfill.

Managing Promises

Once you know what your customers do and don't expect—the promises you will be called on to keep—you are in a position to shape your customers' expectations to match what you actually can and will do for them. When you do that well, customers perceive that you and your company are reliable.

Let's say you are a salesperson in a store selling custom-built personal computers. Bill Smith comes in looking for a four-PC networked system for a small office. He's never purchased custom-built computers before, and assumes—has an expectation—that you have most models in stock and that

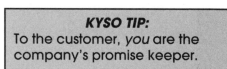

KYSO TIP:
To the customer, *you* are the company's promise keeper.

he'll be able to take his purchase back to the office today. Your challenge is to change his expectations to match what your organization can do for him.

You show your organization's promise—its commitment to quality products—by leading him to several sample systems on the show floor. You reinforce the organization's message with a personal promise: "Our custom systems allow us to combine the features that best meet your needs with the highest quality craftsmanship. If we can finalize the design today, I can have your system delivered and installed in two weeks."

Now Bill has a clear understanding of your promise. He may decide that the wait is worth it because of the quality involved. If he really needs the system today—in which case, you can't change his expectations *this* time—at least he will leave your store knowing the difference between custom made and off the shelf, and knowing that you are concerned with his satisfaction. And he may recommend you to a friend or colleague based on his revised understanding of your capabilities.

Suppose you've worked with Bill to create the expectation that his system will be installed in two weeks. Suddenly you learned that deliveries are running about three days behind schedule. If you don't call with the bad news, you can bet he'll call you when the system doesn't arrive on the day he was told to expect it—and he won't be happy about the delay. On the other hand, if you take the initiative, you might discover that the delay is acceptable. Or, if he has an important project at risk

> **KYSO TIP:**
> Never overpromise just to get the sale. For today's customer, your relationship doesn't end with the sale, it just begins. Keeping the promises you make and only making promises you can keep are what reliability is all about.

if the system doesn't arrive, you can arrange for a loaner until the order arrives. Then, you and your company look like heroes.

Assurance

Your words and actions must *assure* your prospects that they are doing business with a well-trained, skillful professional. Customers know they can trust you because of the competence and confidence you display in your work and in your company.

Today, customers expect to be reassured by the people they deal with. And that takes more than a shoeshine and a smile. It's the combination of style and substance that wins accolades and orders.

Knock Your Socks Off Sales professionals know that trying to get by without an "at-your-fingertips" mastery of your products and services has profound consequences. One study on retailing reports that customers identify "salespeople who know less about their products than I do" as a leading reason for switching from department store to catalog shopping. Another study on the automobile industry finds that two of three car buyers refuse to return to the same dealership for their next car. Their reasons have little to do with the car itself and more with the games they were subjected to on the showroom floor. Buyers trust and return to do business with knowledgeable professionals.

This is why Knock Your Socks Off Selling has such a positive impact on your company, on your customer, and on your career. Self-assured, knowledgeable salespeople stand out, so make yourself memorable.

The Reassurance Factor

Assurance—being reassuring to prospects and customers—is about managing your customers' feelings of *trust*. The customer's decision to trust you is built on your knowledge and know-how. It is the substance that backs up your style, and it comes in four packages:

1. **Product knowledge.** Customers expect you to know the features, advantages, and benefits of whatever it is your company makes, does, or delivers. The salesperson who has to read the manual in front of the customer just to figure out how to turn on the stereo doesn't create an impression of competence.
2. **Company knowledge.** Customers expect you to know more than the limits of your particular job. They expect you to know how your organization works so you can guide them to someone who can meet their needs if they should fall outside your area of responsibility. Can you help your customer navigate the briar patch that is your business easily and successfully? Do you preview your organizational savvy during your sales presentations?
3. **Listening skills.** Customers expect you to listen, understand, and respond to their specific needs as they explain them to you. They expect you to ask pertinent questions that help them do a better job of giving you the information you need to work for them effectively. And they expect you to pay attention and get it right so they don't have to repeat it.
4. **Problem-solving skills.** Customers expect that you will be able to recognize their needs as they express them and quickly align them with the services and products your organization provides. And when things go wrong or don't work, they expect you to know how to get things fixed.

Extra Points for Style

A competent annual physical, performed by a rude, disheveled, or distracted physician isn't likely to be a satisfying experience for the patient, regardless of the technical excellence of the practitioner. Once you've mastered the fundamentals of competence, it's your confident style that sets you apart. It starts with first impressions. In their book, *Contact: The First Four Minutes*, Leonard and Natalie Zunin contend that "the first four minutes of any contact is a kind of audition." In some sales situations, you may have far less time than that.

But first impressions are only the beginning. In sales, everything communicates your style to customers. The way you dress, the way you move, or whether you move at all. The way you talk, the way you do or don't make eye contact, listen, and respond. The way you act when you're not taking care of customers, but still within their view. All these impressions add up to say, "I know what you need. I can take care of that for you."

Tangibles

Selling is difficult to describe in tangible, physical terms. It's fuzzy. Mushy. Slippery. You can't put a yardstick to advice from a stockbroker or ideas from an interior decorator. Twenty minutes with a physician or auto mechanic isn't necessarily better or worse than ten or thirty minutes. It's the quality of what is accomplished, not the quantity of the time involved.

In every sales encounter, there are tangibles—before, during, and after the fact—that affect the way prospects judge you. If a prospect asks for an explanation of your products and you give it, that's intangible. Using diagrams and printed materials is tangible.

Demonstrating Value

Tangibles help convey the value of your selling proposition. They're an important way for you to educate your customers and help them evaluate the quality of your offering—and your company. Manage the tangible aspects of the sales encounter and you give your customers something solid to tie their impressions to.

The best rule of thumb regarding the tangibles you manage is: Never give something to customers you'd be reluctant, embarrassed, or angered to receive yourself. Here are three ways you can demonstrate value:

> **KYSO TIP:**
> If you're helping a customer estimate the cost of a purchase, be it a new stereo or a roomful of carpet, write your calculations neatly on a page with your name and phone number. Your customer will appreciate having it as a reference and will easily remember who provided assistance.

1. Take pride in your own appearance and the look and feel of the materials you give to your customer. Hand them over personally instead of tossing them on a desktop or leaving it to the customer to figure out what to gather up and how to organize and carry them.

2. When customers give you their name, phone number, or other information, write it down. This demonstrates that you think the information is important. And make a point of getting it right—read it back to make sure there's no mistake.

3. Make sure the parts of your workplace the customers see—and especially those they touch—are clean, safe, and as comfortable as you can make them. If you work out of a briefcase, make sure its of good quality. If you drive to customers, keep your car clean, inside and out, and well running.

Empathy

Customers come in a wide variety of shapes and sizes, and they bring an equally wide variety of wants, needs, expectations, attitudes, and emotions with them to the sales transaction. Customers want to be treated as individuals. No one likes to be treated like a number.

Consider how you might treat these two very different customers if you were the banquet manager—the person who sells big events—for a fancy hotel:

- Tom Timid walks into the catering office looking nervous and tense. He is planning a special retirement party for his boss of ten years and he's obviously never organized a function like this before.
- Demanding Doris is an old hand at hosting special events. The annual sales department gala will be the fourth major event she has organized this year. When she walks into the banquet office, Doris knows exactly what she wants. Her you-all-just-stand-back-and-take-orders attitude is clearly visible.

How do you treat Tom and Doris as individuals? For Tom, it is important to make him comfortable and take the time to make him "feel smart" about the event planning process:

"Tom, you can depend on me to be there every step of the way. To begin with, why don't you tell me a little bit more about your event, and then I'll show you our step-by-step planning process."

The same technique would probably frustrate, possibly even anger, Doris. She may see your friendly, in-depth explanation as a waste of her valuable time. She expects you to credit her with the savvy she has shown in previous programs:

"Hello, Doris. It's good to work with you again. I see you brought an outline of everything you need. Let me take a look and see if I have any questions."

Seeing—and treating—each customer as an individual helps you meet the needs of each on his or her own unique level. Showing empathy for customers allows you to be professional and caring at the same time. It also makes customers feel like important individuals. Empathy cannot be handed out by a machine; it's something one person does for another.

Responsiveness

Timeliness has always been important. And today, responsive action—doing things in a timely fashion—is even more crucial. Just look around at the number of businesses that have been created to get things done quickly:

- Federal Express won international success by delivering letters and small parcels "Absolutely, Positively, Overnight."
- LensCrafters optical stores promise "Custom-Crafted Eyeglasses in About an Hour."
- Domino's became America's largest pizza company by meeting a thirty-minute or $3.00 off guarantee. A guarantee that since has been rescinded to ensure the safety of their drivers, but that set a standard for the food delivery industry.

Companies that cater to time-conscious customers are everywhere you look. And their success affects your customers' expectations of your willingness and ability to do the same. Small wonder that your customers are demanding tighter deadlines and faster service than ever before.

Setting—and Meeting—Deadlines

Sometimes it seems that everybody wants everything done at the same time. But it's a mistake to think your customers won't accept anything less than "right this instant," just as giving yourself too much extra "wiggle room" can make you look slow and leave you and your company lagging in the race for a customer's business.

Start by finding out what the customer really needs. There's a big difference between "I have to have this system next week" and "I want to have it in place this fall." Use that information to pick a time that works well for you and try it out on the customer. Nine times out of ten, you'll hear "yes". And if your suggestion doesn't work, your customer will let you know and you can work together to find an alternative—evidence of responsiveness that customers appreciate and remember.

Deadlines are important. But deadlines are created. When you say to a customer, "I'll have it ready for you this afternoon" or "I'll put it in the mail today," you are creating an expectation for your customer and setting a deadline for yourself. Be realistic, because once created, deadlines become yardsticks by which your customer will measure your success or failure. Customer trust results from creating acceptable, realistic expectations of responsiveness, and then meeting those expectations.

> **KYSO TIP:**
> The next time you're in doubt, ask your customers, "When would you like this?" You may be pleasantly surprised when they pick a reasonable time, or even ask you, "Well, when could you have it done?" An added benefit is that it gives them a sense of control and involvement. We are all more comfortable when we feel we have some control over our lives and the things that go on around us.

When Customers Must Wait

The best time for anything is the time that is best for the customer. But dissatisfaction isn't measured in minutes. Rather, dissatisfaction often is the result of uncertainty. Research shows that the most frustrating aspect of waiting is *not knowing how long the wait will be.*

Think about your own experiences as a customer. When you are in line behind someone who insists on paying off the national debt in pennies or are waiting for the manufacturer to plant and grow the oak trees to make your new furniture, it is the uncertainty—Will I have it sometime this century?—more than the wait itself that gets your blood pumping.

> **KYSO TIP:**
> Pay special attention to waiting time when your customers are out of your sight, whether on the phone, in another part of town, or in another state, rather than standing right in front of you.

12

The Presentation:

Telling Your Story, Making Your Case

The old adage is, "It's not what you say—it's how you say it." Wrong. In sales it's both. Making a great sales presentation is a marriage of "what you say" and "how you say it."

The *what* needs to be in hand before there is a *how* to consider. The information you gather on the prospect and the prospect's need, the qualifying questions you asked, and your knowledge of the ins and outs of your product or service form the what. So too are a well-practiced set of answers to the five most common objections to buying. Let's put that in bold so there is no question about its importance:

> **Know your products and services cold and have great answers to the five most common objections down pat.**

Once the *what* is well in hand it's time to focus on the *how* of a successful presentation. There are two extremes to the conduct of a sales presentation. There is the *discovery* presentation and the *solicited* presentation.

The *discovery* presentation is more characteristic of the sales rep approach to selling. A prospect agrees to give you a hearing. You show up with your shoes shined, your hair combed, and your presentation well practiced and memorized. You ask questions, make assertions, trial close the sale, answer objections, final close the sale—and write up the order. Think of it as the "walk in–walk out" presentation, if you like.

The *solicited* presentation is the result of several phases of activity and culminates in a presentation focused on a highly specific, detailed proposal. The process of getting to an order often looks like this:

1. Multiworld Systems announces that it is in search of a new supplier of widgets to its entire eight-country, twenty-facility operation.
2. Six companies, including Acme Widgets, are asked to make capabilities presentations.
3. After the capabilities presentations, three of the six are invited to respond to an RFP—Request for Presentation—and submit a proposal.
4. Acme and the other two are allowed to visit two Multiworld sites, observe operations, and talk with site personnel about their widget wants and needs.
5. Acme and the other two "candidates" are each allotted a block of time to make a presentation and present their proposal. Often, the presentations are scheduled back to back.
6. The Multiworld decision-making team discusses the presentations and proposals, then picks a winner.

This process can take days, weeks, and even months. Not all solicited presentations are this complex, but all involve an RFP of some form, competitors, a proposal, and more than one decision maker.

Most selling opportunities today are less complex than the solicited presentation and more complex than the discovery presentation—although both most certainly exist in abundance. Regardless of the complexity and number of steps and stages, every customer presentation shares four critical elements:

1. **Find the need.** The prospect's need for your product or service has to be determined. In the discovery presentation, the need often is determined on the spot with the

prospect. In the solicited presentation, the need usually is ascertained independently of the proposal presentation.

2. **Determine elemental importance.** Not all aspects of a product or service offering have the same weight to a prospect. For some, price is the critical decision factor; for others it is quality over everything else. In the discovery presentation, importance often is determined via give and take during the presentation. In the solicited presentation, it usually is determined prior to the proposal presentation.

3. **Establish rapport.** Whether dealing with a single prospect or a decision-maker team, putting people at ease, involving them in the sales process, and establishing a personable environment is an important lubricant for a sales presentation.

4. **Build confidence.** In both the discovery presentation and the solicited presentation, you must create confidence in yourself and in your organization. The prospect must be confident that your company can deliver and that you will be on the spot to pitch in when things go wrong.

The Elements of a Knock Your Socks Off Presentation

Even within the two extreme contexts we just described, the one-shot discovery presentation and the multistage solicited presentation, there are a multitude of ways to go with a presentation. No two sales presentations are exactly the same. Every customer, every situation, every deal is unique in some way. Making a presentation is complex, even if you are selling something as simple as a paper clip. Making a winning presentation takes a delicate touch, even if you are selling eighteen-wheel trucks. The words you choose, the attitude you display, and the perceptions you create are critical. The following 21.5 elements of a Knock Your Socks Off sales presentation are not about the structure of your content or the look of your visuals and support material. They are about the process of making your presentation. Not every one of the 21.5 elements applies equally to the discovery and the solicited presentation. But the majority are critical elements to understand, prepare for, and manage if your are going to make a Knock Your Socks Off, order-winning, presentation.

1. Get to the purpose of your visit right away.

"Mr. Smith, my objective today is to show you how Acme widgets can save you money and improve the quality of your finished products."

The prospect wants to know your motive for being in his or her office—even if this is a solicited presentation to a decision-making team. The purpose or benefit statement focuses the prospect's attention on the elements you have determined are most important to Mr. Smith. The sooner you state the purpose, the more relaxed the atmosphere becomes. Once you've stated your purpose, you can digress to rapport building.

2. Establish a friendly and comfortable atmosphere before beginning the presentation. Don't start selling without warming up. Even when you know everyone in the room well. Establish some commonality and rapport. If they don't like you—or remember that you are human or ok—they won't buy from you. It's fine to use personal information as long as you do so carefully. Say you find out the prospect is a sailor. It's ok to say:

"Mr. Smith, you're an avid sailor, aren't you? Is that a picture of your boat?"

Be careful to be seen as interested and friendly, not prying.

3. Be the most positive, most enthusiastic person on the face of the earth (or at least in the meeting). Warm the prospect up to you. Positive attitude and enthusiasm are contagious (and attractive). An "up" atmosphere is a buying atmosphere. Let your desire to help shine through.

"Mr. Smith, I'm really pleased you were able to give me this time. I know I can make the investment of it worth your while."

Caution: Judgment counts. If you are selling funerals—happy talk is out. If you are selling to a company and the prospect(s) see their situations as grave or threatening, ditto. Let the tone and temper of the prospect tell you how up you can afford to be.

4. **State how your product or service will help the prospect.** Do not lapse into a laundry listing of facts and features. Stay focused on benefits and solutions to established problems.

   "Mr. Smith, the 22-K widget cuts your need for expensive overinventory and subcomponent quality checks."

   Tell prospects things about how your product or service solves problems and works on the job. How it works to serve their customers if it is an industrial sale. People don't care what your product does—unless it benefits them. Start with the attitude "I'm here to help," not "I'm here to sell."

5. **Build confidence, trust and credibility as you go.**

   "Mr. Smith, Acme has been supplying companies like yours with widgets for over twenty years. I believe I can show you why Multiworld should use Acme as well."

   Prospects are universally concerned with your ability to get the job done. They gain confidence from your confidence and your promises of proof.

6. **Use power phrases and the buzzwords in your industry.** Using the right language gives the prospect the confidence that you understand the product—and his

business. Powerful positive phrases send the message that buying is safe and secure.

"Acme widgets have been singled out recently for cycle-to-cycle reliability by Widgets Monthly magazine. We were honored by that, but, more importantly, I can show you how that characteristic can benefit Multiworld and your objectives."

7. **Tell the prospect "why we're different," instead of "who we are."** If a prospect is buying a copier, he thinks they're all the same. Show him he's wrong. At the same time, don't use the word "competition" or make competitive comparisons—unless you have to. Substitute the words "industry standard" instead. Get creative, not dirty. Talking about the competition in a derogatory manner never plays well.

"Acme widgets clearly are setting a new standard for quality in the industry. Our copy quality approaches printer quality and our hardware talks to all your PCs."

8. **Position your assertions in terms of "you" and "your," not "me," "I," or "we."** Language and syntax set the tone for the sale. Be sure the tone you set is one that takes the perspective of the only person that matters, the prospect. Talking in terms of "you" automatically sets that tone.

"Mr. Smith, you will be amazed at the price–value balance of the 22-J widget. It will pass all our tests for durability and lower your down time at least 17 percent."

9. **Ask intelligent questions.** The easiest way to build confidence and gain trust is through insightful questions. Identify needs, get important information, create interest, gain confidence, quality affordability, establish credibility, and close the sale all stem from asking questions. Your Power Questions must be preplanned and prewrit-

ten for maximum benefit. It's hard to make up a high-quality Power Question on the spot.

10. **Focus on the value of what you offer and how that meets the prospect's needs.** Forget price—show cost, demonstrate value, list comparisons, prove benefits. Never go into a presentation without a value proposition. Insist your company's marketing department create a value worksheet for you to use. If you cannot appeal to the prospect in a way that's different or sets you apart from others, you'll never close this or any sale. Yes, you can become the default supplier through cost, but is that actually an alternative?

11. **Move quickly through your presentation, but be sure you're understood.** Don't assume the prospect knows what you *should* or *could* have said. Your prospect is hearing this for the first time (even though it may be your 1,000th). Cover every basic aspect of your presentation. Balance that with the fact that our society is getting less patient. It is estimated that by the year 2000, the average prospect will have about a twenty-minute window of attention.

> **KYSO TIP:**
> An age-old presentation structure can help ensure that the prospect will hear what you need them to hear—and remember.
> - Tell'em what you're going to tell 'em.
> - Tell'em.
> - Tell'em what you told 'em.

12. **Take notes.** This may sound terribly minute and too obvious to be mentioned, but we're amazed at how few salespeople take notes or review them with the prospect. Taking notes says "I'm interested in you and what you have to say is important." It also gives you the information you need to make perfect follow-ups, write contracts and proposals, and do accurate deliveries.

13. **Involve the prospect.**
Test him, let him do the demonstration, let him help you set up. The sooner you gain involvement, the easier it is to gain prospect understanding and confidence. Letting them touch the product creates an early sense of ownership.

> **KYSO TIP:**
> If you are dealing with a small part or small device—even a complex diagram of a service—bring it back under your control after the prospect has inspected it. It cuts down on the "fiddle with" factor.

14. **Use testimonials when the time is right.** Testimonials are the best proof you've got. Use them to overcome doubts, objections, stalls, or specific issues that are blocking the sale. Use them one by one. The next best things to testimonials are references to similar situations. "Just last

week we had the same situation with a customer just like you…" A similar situation should reference someone who decided to buy and who the prospect can contact to verify your claims.

15. **Ask approval questions to gain understanding.** Gaining approval on small points along the way leads to getting approval at the end. Questions like:

"Don't you agree?"
"Do you see how this helps?"

Making a benefit statement sets a tone of approval. Even short interrogations like "Isn't it?" or "Doesn't it?" set a tone of "yes" in the mind of the prospect throughout the presentation.

16. **Learn to recognize buying signals.** Usually revealed in the form of a question about price, delivery, specific features, or productivity. Close when you hear them. Don't answer with yes or no. If you do, you go past the sale.

17. **Overcome objections before they occur.** It doesn't matter what product or service you sell, there are only five to ten major objections a prospect can raise and you've heard them all before. Anticipate them, and address them in your presentation, before the prospect has a chance to raise them.

Caution: If you know in advance that a specific objection is a hot button for the prospect, you might choose to let him or her voice it so you can thank him or her for the question and acknowledge its importance before you answer it.

18. **Don't close the sale. Assume the sale.** Assume you have it from the moment you enter the room. Then take the logical steps to complete the transaction. The sale is

a given if the need is present and the presentation is superior.

OK—you do have to ask for the order. And doing a trial close—testing the water as you go—is closing. But your attitude should be that the sale is a lock. Use phrases like "Once we start delivery you'll see how easy these are to store," and "as your experience with our widgets grows, our engineers will be able to show you shortcuts that will further decrease your down time for changeover."

19. **Close the sale all the way.** Handling the details and confirming the next action set the sales as a "done deal." State what you need to get started making deliveries or inaugurating the service. Make an appointment to review and begin. Handle the last detail between the prospect saying "yes" and actually taking ownership on the spot if you can. It cements the decision.

20. **Sell the timely payment for your product or services rendered.** Don't make half a sale. You must also sell financial arrangements and when and how payment is expected. It's incredible to us how many salespeople are afraid to ask for the money. Yet the financing details often are critical to the deal.

21. **Be different.** Just for fun, Jeffrey often tries (without asking) to get the buyer to stand and walk around (he walks around first)—then he sits in the prospect's chair behind the prospect's desk. He usually gets a surprised look, most times a laugh or a smile—and has never had a negative response. It doesn't work for everyone—but we dare you to try it once!

21.5 **Be funny and have fun.** Most people have no fun at work. If you're fun and funny, you'll have an attraction and an advantage. "Make me laugh and you can make me buy" is a credo you can take to the bank. Laughing all the way.

Managing You

We've already discussed the importance of managing the tangibles of dealing with your customers and prospects (Chapter 11) and why those tangibles need to be managed carefully. During a presentation there are only two tangibles—your product samples and literatures and you, yourself.

Until your prospect becomes a customer, you are the embodiment of the company. Whether a customer's feelings about the company are good or bad relates directly to his or her experience with you. Each interaction between the prospect and you makes a positive or negative impression. There is very little neutral or in-between impact. Prospects take in every move, gesture, and nuance of your presentation and evaluate—predict—what the future as a customer of your company would be like. It may not be reasonable or rationale behavior, but it's really all the prospect has to go on.

Here are twenty-one tips for making sure that you are a positive presence when you are in front of the prospect—and that your presentation gets the hearing it deserves.

- **Speak clearly**. Sounds simple, but if the prospect doesn't understand you (accent, dialect, speak too fast, jump around), your communication won't be understood. You also won't get the sale.
- **Lean forward**. Lean into the presentation to give the prospect the sense of importance and urgency.
- **Don't fidget**. Knuckle cracking, pocket jingling, or other nervous habits detract from the presentation.
- **Don't fumble**. Fumbling around means you're not prepared. It makes the prospect feel on edge and act impatient. It also makes him unsure of you and, therefore, unsure about your company, your product, and your service.
- **Don't "um," "ah," or "er."** Vocalized pauses, hesitations, and repeated words are so irritating, they make the prospect focus on the flaws rather than the message. The biggest cure for this is practice.
- **Be animated**. Wide eyed, as though you just had the most fantastic thing just happen to you.

- **Use lots of hand gestures**. Not wild hand waving, but pointed compelling gestures. Pantomime (act out) the words as you speak.
- **Use a wide range of vocal variety**. Loud and soft voices. Not singing, but close. Go from high to low tones. Punch the critical words. Compel the prospect to listen. Say it with style.
- **Whisper some important stuff as if it were a secret**. Get the prospect to lean into your words. Make him or her feel special to get this message.
- **Stand up when you present**. It adds impact to your gestures and to the story (even if you're on the phone).
- **Stand up (sit up) straight**. Posture determines the direction of your words. If you're stoop shouldered, your words are spoken to the floor, instead of to the prospect.
- **Look them in the eye**. Your eye contact is a tell-tale sign of credibility to the prospect. Use direct eye contact. Looking the other person in the eye is a confidence builder.
- **Take presentation risks**. Don't present in a shell. Say new things. Invent new methods of presentation on the spot. If may mean that you get a bit uncomfortable, but so what? That's how you grow.
- **Stay within the range of the prospect's personality**. If the prospect is stuffy or conservative, don't get too wild.
- **Say it with conviction**. The prospect must buy you before he buys your product or service. Your self-belief will account for a large portion of the sale.
- **Select the right words**. Sound intelligent. You don't have to quote Shakespeare, but you do need to be a wordsmith. Use the prospect's industry buzzwords. Build ten new words into your vocabulary every week. No swearing, no matter what. (Even if the prospect swears, you have a professional standard to maintain.)
- **Emphasize important words**. When you come to a critical word or phrase—punch it and pause to let it sink in.
- **Use your entire body to sell**. Gesture with your hands and arms. Get up and walk around the room. Shift your weight for emphasis of a point.

- **Nod yes**. This small subliminal body language technique is among the most powerful in sales. It sets a mood of "yes" throughout the presentation.
- **Smile.** This isn't brain surgery, it's helping other people. It's fun. Your facial expression of a smile makes the prospect feel good inside.
- **Relax**. High anxiety makes the prospect nervous too. The main reason salespeople are nervous is that they are unprepared or they need the money they're about to make if the sale is completed. Calm down. Never let them see (or feel) you sweat.

13

Closing Is a Process, Not a Single Action

You can have the best presentation in the world, you can be an expert in your product or your field of endeavor, but if you don't know how to close the sale, dining out for you will probably always involve more cardboard containers than bone china and Waterford crystal.

Selling experts from Zig Ziglar to J. Douglas Edwards and Earl Nightingale universally agree on the need—and nature—of the close, and even on the definition:

A question whose answer confirms the sale.

There are dozens—if not thousands—of ways to close, to ask for the sale, but they all share a common attribute—they are designed to make it difficult for the prospect to say no in response. Oh, you might not get a yes either, but a well-constructed closing question makes it difficult for the prospect to give you a flat-out no. At worst, it gives you an objection to work with that you eventually can lead to a new close that will garner a yes.

Three Kinds of Closes

Three of our favorite closes are *The Choice,* the *Puppy Dog,* and the *Dessert First.*

The Choice Close

The Choice Close is an assumptive close. It *assumes* the prospect has already decided to buy and there are only details to be worked out.

> *"Mr. Jones would you like those t-shirts in light or dark colors?"*

> *"Mr. Jones, would you like delivery before or after the first of next month?"*

> *"Ms. Smith, did you want to receive that via regular or expedited delivery?"*

Caution: The Choice Close only works when you have confirmed the prospect's interest and have heard concrete buying signals before you deliver it.

For instance: It's Thursday afternoon. Ms. Smith says, "The office is lost without a copy machine. We need to replace this clunker as fast as we can." She hasn't said you're the one yet, but you certainly have enough to offer a close. "Ms. Smith, would it help if we could deliver you a new copy machine Monday morning?"

If you're feeling a little tentative, say, Smith's copy machine isn't dead, just ailing, and she doesn't sound as if she's definitely decided to replace it: "This machine is probably on its last legs. I need to think about replacing it, I suppose." You can turn your close tentative as well—it's called a *trial close*.

> *"Ms. Smith, if I could show you how to replace your current copier with a new one and lower your machine operating costs, would you seriously consider replacing it before it completely breaks down and leaves you stranded?"*

Note: The trial close is a conditioned statement—very conditional. If Smith was carefully qualified, she's very unlikely to turn you down.

The Puppy Dog Close

The easiest way to sell a puppy is to give it to the prospective owner (and the kids) overnight "to see how they like it." Just try to get that puppy away from the kids the next morning. Thus, the name Puppy Dog Close. It is an incredibly powerful sales tool that is used (with variation) by sales professionals around the world.

Think about it for a moment.

- Test drive the car.
- Thirty-day free trial membership.
- Try this in your home for seven days.
- First issue of the magazine is free.
- Two-day demo of our copier in your office.

All these are forms of the Puppy Dog Close.

We're telling the prospect, "This product is great but you may not know it until you touch it, try it, take it home, or use it." If you can get the prospect to touch and/or try your product, you are more likely to get him to buy it.

It's ownership before the sale. It breaks down resistance to the point of acceptance.

You can enhance the use of this tool with the words "if you qualify." This means you can determine if the prospect can afford your product before he or she tries it out. Then if they want to keep it, financing is prearranged.

Obviously not all businesses can use the Puppy Dog Close, but more and more corporate sales strategies call for trying to get their product into the hands of the buyer for a test or trial as part of the selling process. They know statistically that the sale is more likely to be made if the prospect can take ownership before he or she actually commits to the sale.

When you try on a new suit or dress, before you actually make the purchase, you see yourself owning it—the fit, the feel, the look, and the salesperson chortling about how good it looks are often more influential than the price. You can almost see yourself at the office or trade show in your new clothing, then you say, "Ok, I'll take it."

If you doubt the power of this close, go to a pet store and ask them if you can have a puppy overnight for the evaluation. You might want to take your checkbook along, just in case.

The Eat Dessert First Close

You're at one of those banquets where they put out the salad and dessert before anyone arrives. So, when you sit down, you immediately eat the dessert. People are anywhere from surprised to shocked. If they make a comment, ask if they're gong to eat theirs. If they say no, ask them to pass it over.

If someone gives you a choice of apple pie and ice cream or lima beans…. Dessert is to eating as closing is to selling. It's the best part. Tradition says do it last—we say do it first.

Begin to close the sale within ten seconds of entering a prospect's office. State the objective of the meeting and tell the prospect what you would like to do. Tell them you have three strategies of business.

- I'm here to help.
- I seek to establish a long-term relationship.
- I'm going to have fun.

Stating your objective and philosophy at the outset puts the prospect at ease. It gets the meeting off to a great start. It establishes credibility and respect. And it clears the way for a meaningful information exchange and rapport building.

- Tell the prospect what you want when you walk in the door.
- Ask for the sale as soon as you hear the first buying signal.

But First...

Before you can close the sale, you need to know that the client is ready to have you pop the question. You need to have a *buying signal*. Listen closely and the prospect will tell you he or she is ready to be closed.

The buying signal frequently comes in the form of a question. "Do you have different colors in stock?" is a dead giveaway that the prospect is more than a little interested. So is the prospect turning to a spouse or colleague and saying, "We could do a lot with that, couldn't we?"

Here are a baker's dozen plus one, sure-fire signals that the prospect is ready to move toward a decision.

Questions about availability or time.

"Are these in stock?"

"How often do you receive new shipments?"

Questions about delivery.

"How soon can someone be here?"

"How much notice do I have to give you?"

Specific questions about rates, prices, or statements about affordability.

"How much does this model cost?"

"What is the price of this fax machine?"

"I don't know if I can afford that model."

Any questions or statements about money.

"How much money would I have to put down to get this?"

Positive questions about your business.

"How long have you been with the company?"

"How long has your company been in business?"

Wanting something important repeated.

"What was that you said before about financing?"

Statements about problems with previous vendors.

"Our old vendor gave us poor service. How quickly do you respond to a service call?"

Questions about guarantee or warranty.

"How long is this under warranty?"

Specific product or service questions.

"How does the manual feed operate?"

"Do you select the person or do I?"

Specific statements about ownership of your product or service.

"Would you provide paper each month automatically?"

"Will you come by each month to pick up my accounting?"

"Suppose I like her and want her to work for me full time?"

Questions to confirm unstated decision or seeking support.

"Is this the best way for me to go?"

Wanting to see a sample or demo again.

"Could I see the fabric samples again?"

Asking about other satisfied customers.

"Who are some of your customers?"

Asking for a reference.

"Could I contact someone you did temp work for using Lotus Notes and WordPerfect?"

"Do you have a list of references?"

Responding to the Buying Signal

There is an interim step between hearing the buying signal and delivering a close. You have to answer the buying signal question. The craft is to do it in a way that moves you a step closer to the sale, that sets up the closing question. An effective approach is to answer a buying signal question with a confirming question. Sound complicated? Not really. Not once you've seen it in action.

Here are some examples of confirming questions.

Q: *"Do you have this model?"*
A: *"Is this the model you want?"* If the prospect says yes, all you have to do now is find out when he wants delivery and you're finished.

Q: *"Does it come in green?"*
A: *"Would you like it in green?"*

Q: *"Can you deliver on Tuesday?"*
A: *"Is Tuesday the day you need it delivered?"*

Q: *"Are these in stock?"*
A: *"Do you need immediate delivery?"*

Q: *"What is your delivery lead time?"*
A: *"How soon do you need delivery?"*

Q: *"How much notice do I have to give you?"*
A: *"How much notice do you usually have?"*

Q: *"How soon can someone be here?"*
A: *"How soon do you need someone here?"*

You can also answer directly and still pose a closing question immediately thereafter. For example:

Q: *"When will the new model be out?"*
A: *"January 30th. But we have special incentives to take the copier now. Let's compare which will be the best way for you to go. Fair enough?"*

Q: *"Do you have references?"*
A: *"Here is the list. If our references are satisfactory, when would we be able to get our first assignment?"*

Here's the Formula

1. Recognize the buying signal when you see it.
2. Construct a confirming question or give an answer that leads to another question.
3. Deliver the response in smooth, fairly casual money. Don't pounce.

The Five-Question Close

We've emphasized several times the power of good questions. Nowhere is this more apparent than in the close. Jeffrey reconstructed the following five-question closing sequence based on his actual experience that shows that power. In spades. The salesperson is selling a simple mundane product—printing. But the five-question sequence is pure Knock Your Socks Off Selling.

Question 1: *"Mr. Prospect, how do you select a printer?"*

Prospect: *"Quality, delivery, and price."*

Question 2: *"How do you define quality?"* or *"What does*

quality mean to you?" (ask the same *"how do you define"* question for all three responses of the *"how do you choose"* question.)

The prospect will give you thoughtful answers. Many prospects have never been asked questions like these, and they will be forced to think in new patterns. You may even want to ask a follow-up question or create a tie-down question here before going to Question 3. For example, the prospect says he defines quality as crisp, clear printing. You ask, *"Oh, you mean printing that reflects the image of the quality of your company?"*

How can a prospect possibly say no to that question?

Question 3: *"What makes that important to you?"* or *"Is that most important to you?"* or *"Why is that important to you?"*

This question draws out the true need of the prospect. Finding out what is important to them about printing, and why printing is important, are the keys to closing the sale. There may be secondary or follow-up questions to gain a clear definition of what is important and why.

Question 4: *"If I could deliver the quality you demand so that the image in your printing reflects the image of your business to your customers, and I could do it in the time frame you require, at a reasonable (not the cheapest) price, would I be (variation: is there any reason I would not be) a candidate for your business?"*

Of course you would! This is a feedback question that combines the data found in the first three questions. It's the classic *"If I…, would you"* question that makes the prospect commit. It actually precloses the prospect. If there is a true objection (*"we have to get bids"*… *"Someone else decides"* … *"I'm satisfied with my present vendor"*), it is likely to surface here.

Question 5: *"Great! When could we begin? or "Great! When is your next printing project?"*

The object of the fifth question is to pin the prospect down to a beginning date or time or quantity to start doing business. In many cases you can sell a sample order or trial. Where big-ticket products are involved (copiers, computers), a puppy dog approach will work best (leave your product for the customer to use for a few days), or take the prospect to visit a satisfied customer and see your product in operation and get a live testimonial.

The Tone of the Close

The key to the close is to ask for the sale in a sincere, friendly manner. Don't push or use high pressure. A good close—the right close for the situation—should lead the prospect, not shove him or her, in the direction of "yes."

Self-confidence is important. When you stop talking, when you have asked your closing questions and gone silent, tension will build—quickly.

A minute can seem like an hour when the room is silent. It's not your job to break the silence. The question on the table is there for the prospect to answer. You speak first—and you lose. You've done the prospect's job for her.

The Golden Rule of Closing

After you ask a closing question

SHUT UP!

Self-confidence is of supreme importance in selling. It takes self-confidence to cold call. It takes self-confidence to take on objections. It takes self-confidence to voice a closing question—and shut up. Most salespeople don't ask for the sale because they are afraid of rejection, uncomfortable about money, or don't recognize legitimate, real, buying signals from a customer.

Rule of thumb: Close early and close often. It eases the tension for everyone.

14

Overcoming Objections and Dealing with Doubt

Your presentation was great. You heard clear buying signals. You asked for the order and the prospect said:

"Oh, I'm not sure."

or

"I'm happy with my present supplier."

or

"It's probably too complex for my people."

or

"Nice, but it costs too much."

It would be nice—make that wonderful—if you walked into a customer's office, made your presentation, and were greeted with, "By golly that's great! Just sign us up!" Don't hold your breath waiting. It hardly ever happens.

Objections are, in fact, buying signals. Prospects who don't have qualms and questions, who don't need clarifications and reassurances, have either lost interest and turned you off or have decided to buy and are waiting for you to quit talking and ask for the order.

However you look at objections, as bane or buying signal, you need to recognize one when you hear one and know how to deal with them with tact and efficiency.

Why They Object

Prospects object for a myriad of reasons. Sometimes their objections are exactly what they seem to be. "We can't afford that much" might mean exactly that. Other times objections are a way for the prospect to create thinking space to consider your proposition. Sometimes there is a real objection—not just the one being voiced. Sometimes "It costs too much" is a lot easier to say than "Good Lord! That is the ugliest thing I've ever seen." Sometimes the customer just wants to put you through your paces—see if you can handle the objection. Call that objection raising for entertainment. Not quite like pulling wings off flies for fun, but similar!

And sometimes the prospect is simply second cousin to Oscar the Grouch and has never heard a buying proposition that didn't sound like a Trojan horse to him. Unless you are Sigmund Freud's great-grandchild, you'll probably never really know which objections are real, which are smoke screens, and which are just a part of the prospect's personality.

So the very best policy and philosophy is to:

- **Expect and welcome objections.** Don't over-react. Don't look at the prospect as if he just threatened your puppy. Don't ask him if he's crazy. When it makes sense, you might even smile and thank the prospect for his objection: "I'm glad you brought that up, Bob."

- **Be prepared do deal with it.** The best defensc is—if not a good offense—at least a well-prepared defense. Every time you hear a new objection, write it down and work out an answer.

- **Work to understand the prospect.** Consider the objection a starting point for a new avenue of dialogue with the prospect, an opportunity to put your listening and questioning skills to work. Above all else, be kind and patient.

    If selling were automatic, automatons would be doing it, not you. About 7 percent of last year's holiday shopping took place via the Internet. Another 17 percent was transacted via catalogue. The rest was the product of interaction between a salesperson and a prospect.

Your job—your real job—begins when the prospect objects. It's up to you to patiently, carefully, and skillfully work the prospect through his or her doubts to a sale.

- **Look for the real objection.** Regardless of how valid an objection may sound, it's a good idea to test the reality before mounting a response. Call the following seven steps:

The Cliffs Notes Version of Managing and Overcoming Objections

---

1. **Listen to the objection and decide if it's true.** A prospect usually will repeat an objection if it is real. If you, say, ignore a first price objection, "that must be awfully pricey," and a few minutes later the prospect says, "I like your ideas but we don't have a lot of budget for that sort of thing," you need to stop and let the prospect talk through the objection. You start that process by agreeing, "Mr. Smith, I agree that we aren't the low-price provider. Can you tell me more about why our price is a problem?"

   On the other hand, if you believe that the objection is a stall, you need to get through it before you can continue your presentation. Try one of these for getting at the real objection.

   "You are telling me price is a problem, but could it really be an issue of value?"

   "Sometimes when people tell me price is a problem, there are other problems as well. Is that true here?"

   "Don't you really mean…?"

2. **Once you have the real objection, qualify it as the only true objection.** Question it. Ask the prospect if it is the only reason he or she won't purchase from your company. Ask if there is any other reason he or she won't purchase besides the one given.

3. **Confirm it again, in a different way.** Rephrase your question to ask the same thing twice.

   "In other words, if it wasn't for..., you'd buy my service, is that true, Mr. Johnson?"

4. **Qualify the objection to set up the close.** Ask a question in a way that incorporates the solution

   "So, if I were able to prove the reliability," or *"If I were able to get you extended terms,"* or *"If I were able to show you the system in a working environment, would that be enough for you to make a decision?"* or a variation, *"Would that make me a candidate for your business?"*

5. **Answer the objection so that it completely resolves the issue, and confirm the resolve.** If the objection is real but easily answerable, first agree that it is an issue others have raised. Then use every tool in your box at this point. If you've got trump cards, play them now (a testimonial letter, a comparison chart, a customer you can call on the spot, a special time- or price-related deal).

6. **Answer the objection by asking a closing question, or communicating to the prospect in an assumptive (I have the sale in hand) manner.**

   - *"If I could..., would you"* is the classic model for the close.
   - *"I'm pretty sure we can do this. I have to check one fact with my office—if it's a go on my part, I'm assuming we have a deal."* Or *"I could meet with all the decision makers to finalize it."*

- Use similar situations when you close. People like to know about others in the same situation.
- Ask *"Why is this/that important to you?"* Then use, *"If I could..., would you."*

7. Confirm the answer and the sale in writing.
Get the prospect to convert to a customer with a confirming question like:

- *"When do you want it delivered?"*
- *"When is the best starting day to begin?"*
- *"Is there a better day to deliver than others?"*
- *"Where do you want it delivered?*

An Observation About Objections

There are mountains written about closing and overcoming objections. Our philosophy is to learn as many of these techniques as you can from every book, tape, and seminar available. But, at its heart, overcoming objections isn't about having a bigger bag of tricks than the other person. It's about establishing trust and credibility and ensuring that your prospect clearly sees the value of your proposition.

15

Common Objections—and Their Answers

The seven ideas for overcoming objections from the previous chapter should put you in good stead—regardless of the objection the prospect raises. Knowing the process is as important as having a pocketful of handy answers. Just the same, some objections are so common that there is no sense reinventing the wheel. Here are the three most common, and several ways of dealing with them:

"I want to think about it."

Let's say you're trying to sell Jones Construction a new copier. Jones is interested, but gives you the "think it over" objection.

Perhaps the following will get Mr. Jones off the fence and onto the order pad...

> **KYSO TIP:**
> "Thinking it over" is almost always a stall, not a true objection. You can only make the sale if you find out what the true objection(s) is and creatively overcome it.

Salesperson: Great! Thinking it over means you're interested, correct Mr. Jones?

Jones: Yes, I am.

Salesperson [*said in a humorous vein*]: You're not just saying "I want to think about it" to get rid of me, are you?

Jones [*laughter*]: Oh, no, no, no.

Salesperson [*seriously*]: You know, Mr. Jones, this is an important decision. A copier is not just a duplicating device. Every time you send a copy out to a customer, it reflects your company's image. I'm sure you agree with me. Is there anyone else in your company you will be thinking it over with? (Meaning: Is he deciding alone, or are others involved?)

Jones: No, just me.

Salesperson: I know you are an expert at building; your reputation speaks for itself, but I'm an expert on copiers. In my experience in the copier industry over the past six years, I've found that most people who think things over develop important questions that they may not have answers for. Because the image of your business is on every copy you make, why don't we think it over together so that as you develop questions about the copier, I'll be right here to answer them? Fair enough? Now, what was the main thing you wanted to think about? (At this point, you will begin to get the real objection[s].)

Note: If Mr. Jones had said he was going to think it over with others, you must think it over with all parties in the same room, or you're really at risk.

Fifty percent of the time when a prospect says, "I really want to think it over," it really means he or she:

- Doesn't have the money.
- Can't decide on his own.
- Wants to shop around.
- Doesn't need your product now.
- Has a friend in the business.
- Knows he can buy it cheaper elsewhere.
- Doesn't trust or have confidence in you.
- Doesn't trust or have confidence in your company.
- Doesn't like your product.
- Doesn't like you.

The other 50 percent of the time he will buy. The prospect can be sold if you use the right words or phrases.

"I want to buy, but the price is too high."

Mercedes-Benz is one of the most expensive cars in the world. Some people say, "The price is too high," but they sell thousands of autos worldwide. Mercedes is one of the wealthiest companies in the world.

"The price is too high" has been a cry from buyers since the open market in Damascus, 2000 years ago ... but they still bought.

"The price is too high" is a classic objection. To overcome it you must find out what the prospect actually means. Assuming he or she wants to buy now and the person you're speaking to is the sole decision maker, there are actually five possible meanings behind this objection:

"I can't afford it."

"I can buy it elsewhere cheaper (or better)."

"I don't want to buy from you (or your company)."

"I don't see, perceive, understand the cost or value of your product or service."

"I'm not convinced yet."

About half the time you get a price objection you will not make the sale. That leaves a 50 percent opportunity window. Open it.

Here are some probes you can try:

- **Prove affordability**. "What we will do for you costs less in comparison to what it will cost you if you don't hire us and proceed on your present course."
- **Challenge**. "What are you willing to pay?" "What price can you afford?"

- **Get a feel for the difference.** "How much 'too high' is it?"
- **Talk about value and tomorrow.** "Mr. Jones, you're thinking about pennies per day; we're talking about value over a lifetime."

One That Works Very Well

"Would you buy it from me now [not 'today'] if the price was lower? [Assume the prospect says yes.] You mean other than price, there is no reason we can't do business? [*Note:* You have double qualified the prospect on the price objection to determine it is the real, true, and ONLY objection.] If we can figure a way to make it affordable, will you take delivery [begin/order] right away?"

If the prospect says yes, then you have to creatively figure out a way to change the terms, offer a discount, offer a future credit of items to enhance the value, compare price to cost, or simply resell at the original price. The key is to prepare these answers in advance. You know the objection is coming. Why be surprised?

If the prospect wants your product or service badly enough, he'll figure out a way to afford it. Just because he says the price is too high doesn't mean he won't buy. What is actually being said many times is, "I want to buy. Show me a way.

"I have to talk this over with my ..."

When you hear the words, "I'll have to talk this over with...," you realize you've done something very wrong. You didn't qualify the prospect very well, did you? You probably failed to ask, "Is there anyone else you work with on decisions like this?" Ok, what do you do now?

When others need to approve the deal, besides qualifying the buyer better, you must take four action steps:

- Get the prospect's personal approval.
- Get on the prospect's team.
- Arrange a meeting with all decision makers.
- Make your entire presentation again.

1. **Get the prospect's personal approval.** "Mr. Jones, if it was just you and you didn't need to confer with anyone else, would you buy it?" (The prospect will almost always say yes). Ask, "Does this mean you'll recommend our product to the others?"

   Now, go through a checklist that seems a little redundant but that can uncover any remaining areas of doubt. Ask some version of one or more of these:

   - Is the price OK?
   - Is the product OK?
   - Is the service OK?
   - Is the company OK?
   - Am I OK?
   - What doubts do you have?
   - Do you like it well enough to own it?

Note: Revise these questions to suit what you sell. Revise them in a more personalized way. The objective is to nail down absolute approval. Get the prospect to endorse you and your product to the others, but don't let him (or anyone) make your pitch for you.

2. **Get on the prospect's team.** Begin to talk in terms of "we," "us," and "the team." By getting on the prospect's team, you can get the prospect on your side of the sale.

- **"What do WE have to do?"**
- "When can WE get them together?"
- "When does the team meet next? It's important that I be present because I'm sure they'll have questions that they will want answers to."
- "What can I do to be a member of the team?"
- "Tell me a little bit about the others." (Write down every characteristic.) Try to get the personality traits of the other deciders.

3. **Arrange a meeting with all deciders.** Do it any way you have to. Leave several alternative open times from your date book. Use the alternatives as a reason to get back and solidify your meeting with the decision-making group.

4. **Make your entire presentation again.** You only have to do this if you want to make the sale. Otherwise, just leave it to the prospect. He thinks he can handle it and will try his best to convince you of that.

> **KYSO TIP:**
> The best way for you to make this (or any) sale is to be in control of the situation. If you make the mistake of letting your prospect become a salesperson on your behalf (goes to the others instead of you), you will lose. Every time.

An Alternative Method

Ask the prospect if he's sure the other party (wife, boss) will want to do the deal. If the prospect says, "Yes, I'm sure," you say, "Great! Why not just approve the purchase now (sign the contract) and get their approval? If you call me tomorrow and tell me no, I'll tear up the contract. Fair enough?" The odds are 50/50, so it's worth a try.

16

Objection Prevention:

A New Way to Enjoy Safe Sales

There are no new objections. You've heard them all before. Whatever business you're in, there are between five and twenty reasons why the customer won't buy now on the spot.

Jeffrey swears he knows a first-rate, high-dollar salesperson who will only make appointments with prospects on the condition that they will say either "yes" or "no" at the end of his presentation. They are not allowed to say, "I want to think about it," or he won't make the appointment. A bit wild, maybe even far fetched, but the concept is right.

Prevention is the best way to overcome objections.

Here's how the process works...

1. **Identify all possible objections.** Meet with other sales reps in your organization and even some customers. Brainstorm objections. Ask everyone for the top ten objections they get. They'll flow like water.

2. **Write them down.** Make a detailed list of every objection you have identified. Often the same objection is given in a variety of ways.

3. **Script objection responses with closing questions for each.** It may take some time to complete this task. Do

it with your reps and perhaps a few customers in the room. Create several scenarios for each objection.

4. **Develop sales tools that enhance and support every response.** Items like testimonial letters, comparison charts, and support documentation could enhance the "objection to close" process. Develop whatever you need to make the salesperson feel supported and able to make the sale easier.

5. **Rehearse the scripts in role playing.** After the responses are written, schedule several role-playing sessions to become familiar with each scripted situation and practice until it becomes (and sounds) natural.

6. **Tweak the scripts.** After you role play, there will be revisions to the scripts. Make them immediately.

7. **Try them out on customers.** Go to a favorite customer or two. Tell them what you're doing—they'll be flattered that you had the courage, and they'll most often give you truthful responses. (They may ask for copies for themselves.)

8. **Make final revisions based on real-world situations.** The real world always changes a script or approach. Be sure to document revisions every time you make them.

9. **Keep the documents in a master notebook.** Give all salespeople a copy. There is an added bonus to this system—when you hire a new person, he or she has a training manual that will provide insight and income.

10. **Meet regularly as a group to discuss revisions.** There is always someone inventing the new best way possible.

It's so simple it works.

Here are seven tools for objection prevention to consider adding to your scripts and incorporating into your presentation as part of this process.

1. **Similar situations.** Stories about customers who had the same or similar problem or objection who bought despite of the objection.

> **KYSO TIP:**
> The key is to know the objections that are likely to occur, and script the answers or responses into your regular presentation so that when you come to the close, there's nothing to object to.

2. **Testimonial letters.** Some of them can be closers, for example, "Thought the price was too high, but after a year of lower maintenance cost, I realized the overall cost was actually $20 lower than last year. Thanks for talking me into it."

3. **A story or article in print about the product or your company.** Build support, build credibility, build confidence.

4. **A comparison chart.** Compare the competition's apples to apples and use it when the prospect says he wants to check around.

5. **Say, "Our experience has shown...."** One of the most powerful lead-ins to preventing an objection.

6. **Say, "We have listened to our customers."** It acknowledges that others have voiced this objection, and your company has responded. "They had a concern about..." "Here's what we did..." To get the prospect to see his potential objection disappear, and how you listen and respond.

7. **Say, "We used to believe..., but we have changed and now we..."** Use this as a method of preventing a myth from recurring (reputation for poor service, high price, etc.).

If you can overcome an objection in your presentation before the prospect raises it, you are more likely to make a sale.

Here are two working examples:

- **Preventing price objections....**
  "You know, Mr. Jones, many people told us our price is not competitive, but in our experience we found that the customer was confusing price with cost. Let me show you why we are the lowest cost even though we may not be the lowest price initially." (You then show cost over a two- or three-year period that makes you lower, or a comparison of the cost of after-the-sale services. Let the prospect sell himself on the price after he has been educated about the true cost.)

- **Preventing the "I've got a satisfactory supplier" objection with a testimonial letter....**
  "You know, Mr. Jones, many prospects we call on already have good relationships with one of our competitors. I'd like to share a letter from a customer who felt just like I'm sure you feel. He thought he had a great supplier until he gave us a trial order."
  (Show the letter.)

The Real World...

If you can anticipate objections, you can prevent them from occurring. Sounds simple; it just requires preparation and practice. It takes time, creativity, and focus to make it happen. Please try it. Your reward for superior effort will be superior sales, which leads to superior earnings.

17

How Did That Happen?

The Failed Sales Call Postmortem

You did your homework. You were energetic, positive, charming, well informed, practiced, and polished. You involved the prospect and his staff. You answered all their questions to their satisfaction. As far as you could tell. You think.

And they said, "No."

Or, worse yet, they said, "Let us talk about your proposal with some other people and get back to you. Thanks for coming in." The kiss of death.

What Went Wrong?

There are a number of sales postmortem processes. The best ones look at two factors: your behavior and the prospect's behavior. Or, more precisely, why thy buyer didn't, and what you did that contributed to the "no thank you" decision.

Let's start with the buyer. Let's assume for a minute you had a qualified buyer, someone who could, at least hypothetically, use your product or service. And let's assume that the dollars were or are available. Then the question is, "What didn't happen in the buyer's mind?"

The Four No's Test

A test we like, one we first heard used by sales training guru Larry Wilson, is called:

The Four No's Test

- No trust.
- No need.
- No help.
- No hurry.

The four no's suggest that qualified buyers don't buy from you for one of four reasons:

1. **No trust.** There may indeed be a need, but something about you or your proposal has led the prospect to feel that you—or it—can't meet the need. Salespeople from small companies selling to prospects in large companies encounter this doubt all the time. It's a legitimate fear. One you need to anticipate in your presentation.

2. **No need.** You may not have uncovered a legitimate need. Or you may not have sold the prospect on the idea of the need. It's called denial. Doctors run into it all the time. "Geez, Doc, it's just a headache. Brain surgery! I don't think so."

3. **No help.** Ok, there is a need and it needs to be met. But something about your proposal looks "off" to the prospect. He, she, or they don't see your proposition or product working the wonders you're promising.

4. **No hurry.** There is a need, you have a good idea, and it probably will work. But what's the rush? Somehow, you and the prospect don't see eye to eye on the urgency. The Y2K computer problem didn't seem very immediate to a lot of information technology people—in 1985.

The Three-Speeches Test

A second test involves replaying your presentation and picking it apart—constructively. It comes from a university speech coach who liked to tell his students that the three most important speeches for an aspiring speaker to study are not Lincoln's *Gettysburg Address*, Shakespeare's *"Friends, Romans and Countrymen"* speech from Julius Caesar, and Churchill's *"Blood, Toil, Tears, and Sweat"* speech—as some speaking coaches advise.

Instead, he advised: study the last speech you gave, compared and contrasted with the speech you planned to give, compared and contrasted with the speech you would give now if you could start all over.

Applying this idea to the sale gone wrong really can pay off. Sit down with a copy of your presentation outline and materials, compare the presentation you made with the presentation you planned to give, and *then* compare it with the presentation you would give if you could do it over again.

Let's Unwrap That a Little

1. The presentation you gave probably varied—a little or a lot—from the presentation you planned on making. Write down at least *three things* that did not go as planned.
2. Next, write down at least *three things* you would leave out if you had a chance to do the presentation over again tomorrow.
3. Now write down *three things* you would *add* to the presentation if you were doing it again.

Look at your three lists and see what they tell you about:

- Your prepresentation preparation,
- The content of the presentation you made, and
- The way you delivered your presentation.

These two tests should give you a significant amount of insight into what went wrong.

Twenty-Questions Test

If the Four "No"s and the Three-Speeches tests are too open ended for you—they are for some people—or if you want one more template for giving yourself some feedback, here are twenty specific questions you can use to evaluate your performance and your selling proposition to see where you might have gone astray.

1. Was I on time? Did I show up five minutes early (good) or five minutes late (very bad)?
2. Was I prepared? Did I walk into my appointment with everything I needed to make the sale?
3. Was I organized? Did I have everything at my fingertips or was I fumbling?
4. Could I answer all product questions? Did I really have command of my product or was I constantly saying, "I have to get back to you on that one"?

5. Did I make excuses or blame others about anything? "The sample wasn't shipped on time," "The company didn't send the right information."
6. Was I apologizing? "Sorry I'm late," was unprepared, don't know the answer, didn't bring the correct information, quoted the wrong price, etc.
7. Did the prospect probe personal issues about my company? "If I buy," said Mr. Jones, "how do I know you'll be here to service me in six months?"
8. Did the prospect ask doubting questions about my product? "What happens if it breaks down after the warranty," or "Who else buys this product?"
9. Did the prospect ask doubting questions about me? Such as how long have I been with the company or how much experience I have?
10. Did I name drop other satisfied customers effectively? Did I fail to use the name of a satisfied customer to answer a pointed question?
11. Did I feel as though I was on the defensive? Was I constantly answering questions dealing in subject matters other than my product or service? Could I prove my points?
12. Could I overcome all objections in a confident manner? Did I find myself unable to respond confidently about price, quality, and other issues blocking the sale when asked by the prospect? Did I try to "fake it"?
13. Did I put down the competition? Did I berate my competitor (possibly the prospect's supplier)? Did I make disparaging remarks about the competition to try to make me or my product look better?
14. Was my prospect uninvolved in my sales presentation? Did the prospect just sit there or, worse, do other things while I was talking?
15. Was I too anxious to make the sale? Was I too pushy? Was it obvious to the prospect there was a commission involved?
16. Did my proposal seem on target? Did they seem to need more clarification than others have? Did anyone try to "reexplain" their situation?

17. Did they argue with my facts? Was there ever a moment it seemed the prospect just didn't believe what I was saying?

18. Did the prospect make "future need" statements that I failed to respond to as objections? Things like, "That is something we're going to have to deal with one of these days, all right."

19. Was my energy too low? Did I seem to be walking through my presentation rather than living it passionately?

20. Did the prospect give signals that there was a conflict for his or her time? Was he or she preoccupied? Did I fail to reconfirm that this was a good time for us to be talking?

Seller's Remorse

There is a natural tendency among salespeople all to blame the buyer when things go wrong. "They were just too dumb to appreciate our proposal," or "Her brother-in-law must be in the business. That's the only reason she could have said no!" Hard as it is to accept, there are two undeniable realities in selling:

1. **Not everyone buys from us, even when they should.**

2. **Most of the time, the fault lies within ourselves, not the stars.**

Hanging in tough is the hallmark of the winner. Thomas Edison went through more than 100 unsuccessful versions of the light bulb before he discovered the one that worked. The same thing works in selling—hang in, keep trying, and learn from the ones who go in the ditch. Powerful learnings come from thorough autopsies, difficult as they are to do.

Part Three

Developing and Managing the Long-Term Relationship

The longer a customer is with you, the more profitable your business with his or her company becomes. The longer a customer is with you, the more likely the customer is to buy additional products and services from you. And the longer a customer is with you, the more likely it is that something will go wrong. Your job is to manage that relationship—rain or shine, in sickness and in health—for the long term.

18

"Moments of Truth" in Selling

Customers evaluate you—size you up—a "moment of truth" at a time. A moment of truth can be a casual conversation, a returned phone call, a product presentation, or a smile and a handshake. A moment of truth is any point in your customer's cycle of experience with you and your company that forms a lasting impression—positive or negative—in his or her mind.

Pile up enough **negatives** at those critical moments of truth and the customer loses confidence in you—perhaps cuts you off, or even bids you farewell before you have a chance to make your first proposal. Stack up enough **positives**—at the right moments of truth—and you have a customer for life.

The trick is knowing which encounters, out of the hundreds of contacts you have with prospects and customers, are actually "moments of truth" that make a lasting impression on your customers and prospects and that need your attention and management.

The Big Seven Moments of Truth

We've[1] found that there are seven categories or *types* of moments of truth that salespeople with long-time customers and good relations with their customers have learned to be sensitive to and

1. The big seven moments of truth come from a Performance Research Associates, Inc., study of fifty companies that excel at customer retention. Successfully managing these seven moments of truth accounts for more than 75 percent of the difference between salespeople with a portfolio of long-term customers and those with only a handful of long-term customers.

work hard at managing. These categories of critical moments of truth are:

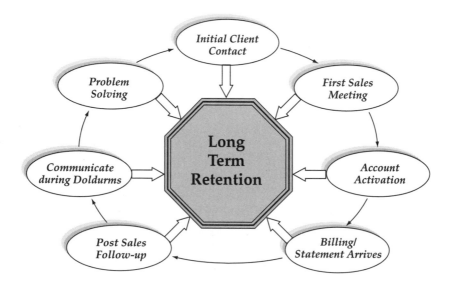

1 **Initial client contact.** Like first impressions on a first date, prospects size you up very quickly. Researchers Arthur and Natalie Zunin contend that a prospect, a new neighbor, a potential employer, or a blind date forms a lasting impression of you within the first four minutes of meeting you. That first contact can be face to face, over the phone, or simply exposure to your company's literature.

2. **First sales meeting.** If the first contact is important, the first sales meeting is doubly so. How you manage that meeting sets the tone for everything that follows. Most important, it tells the prospect how competent you are and what you will be like to do business with.

3. **Account activation.** Up to this point, everything has been hypothetical, a promise of how it will be to do business with you. When the first shipment arrives, the power goes on, the first copy rolls into the print tray, or

the first call for help—this is his or her first taste of the reality of doing business with you.

4. **Billing/statement arrives.** The arrival of the first statement and/or the first bill may not seem a highlight to you as a salesperson, but to the customer it is an opportunity to assess the value of your product or service—and the value of your relationship with the buyer. This is a particularly important moment of truth with purchasing agents.

5. **Post sales follow-up.** Revisiting the customer after the sale is made and the account activated is a "bonus" moment of truth. Coming back to answer questions, reinforce the buying decision, and once again thank the customer for his or her business staves off buyer's remorse and gives you an opportunity to deal with second thoughts before they occur.

6. **Communicating during the "doldrums."** If you only communicate with the customer when one of you needs something, the account is continually at risk. How you use the time between orders or contract renewals cements—or distances—the relationship. Staying in touch with the customer, in meaningful—not trite—ways, is a crucial step in building a long-term relationship

7. **Problem solving.** Today more than ever, the customer expects his or her salesperson to be on top of problems. He or she also expects you to respond when there is a problem to be solved. Today's customer wants as few points of contact with your organization as possible. Preferably just one. You.

Do these moments of truth apply to *every* buyer-seller relationship? Possibly not. The "account activation" moment of truth, for example, has little applicability to retail sales. But in business-to-business selling, all seven apply and have a powerful impact on long-term relations.

Warning! Every customer, every prospect, is a unique individual, with a unique personality and idiosyncratic sensitivities. A moment of truth that one customer places stock in may mean nothing to another customer. Just the same, these seven moments of truth are, on average, where most of the differences between "hello—goodbye" and long-term customer relations will be found. The trick for you as a Knock Your Socks Off salesperson is to learn which of these moments of truth are critical for a given customer and which are not.

The following seven chapters look at these seven moments of truth in selling in more detail and give you the clues you need to know which matter most to your customers and some hints at making them work for you.

19

Moment of Truth One:

Initial Customer Contact

Remember the axiom, "You never get a second chance to make a good first impression"? Well, it's true. And that first impression can be anything from a phone call from a prospect to your office, a brochure that arrives on your prospect's desk, or a cold call from you to a prospect. To make a good first impression you need to know two things:

1. The first impression you are creating now; and
2. The first impression you *want* to make on your prospects.

Step 1: Start by assessing the impression you—and your company—are already making in the marketplace. Here are four assignments that should give you a good picture:

- Have three friends read one or two of your company brochures, something that goes to prospects without any prework. Ask them what impressions (in twenty-five words or less) they have of your company as a result of reading the material.
- Hold an empathy walk. Ask one or more of those three friends to visit your office or place of business.

149

What stands out to them? What don't they even notice? Have one call your office and pose as a prospect. What is that experience like?

- Another way to find out what impression your office makes on your customers and prospects is to go away, call your office, disguise your voice, and ask for some complex information. Write everything down: the number of rings it takes to answer the phone, the impression the answerer makes on you, the difficulty involved in getting the information you asked for—everything. (You might want to follow this up by calling your biggest competitor and asking for the same or similar information.)
- Here's the tough one. Ask those three existing customers what their first impression was of you and your company. (Plan a fifteen- to twenty-minute face-to-face meeting to do this.)

Step 2:   Decide what impression you want to create. Here are two more points to ponder.

   1. What do you want your customer's first impression of your **company** to be?

✔ Quality vendor?	✔ Value oriented?
✔ Lowest cost?	✔ Fastest delivery?
✔ Error-free delivery?	✔ Innovative?
✔ Easy to deal with?	✔ Flexible?

You can't create what you can't state. Once you can articulate the impression you want your company to have in the prospect's mind, review your correspondence, your materials, and the way you and your office look to see if they create this important first impression.

Note: If you want your prospects to see you and your company as crisp and responsive, letting the phones ring off the hook and employing a phone answer person—or service—who sounds like a short-order cook won't get the job done.

   2. What do you want your customer's first impression of **you personally** to be?

✔ Dynamic?	✔ Reserved?
✔ Technical?	✔ Serious?
✔ Good natured?	✔ Original?
✔ Friendly?	✔ Resourceful?

Visualizing the impression you want the initial contact with you and your company to form in the customer's mind and memory is the first step in creating it. Whether the initial contact is with a piece of marketing literature, your receptionist, or you, it is critical to know what you want that impression to be if you are going to be successful at making it happen.

Before Moving On

In the spaces below, write two short sentences or phrases, one describing the way you would like your *company* to be perceived at first contact, and one describing how you would like you *yourself* to be perceived at first contact.

- _____

- _____

The customer buys the salesperson FIRST. The first sale that's made is YOU!

20

Moment of Truth Two:

The First Sales Meeting

Whether your first sales meeting is face to face or phone to phone, it is crucial to orchestrate and manage that encounter for a positive outcome. Think of the successful first sales meeting as a three-legged stool:

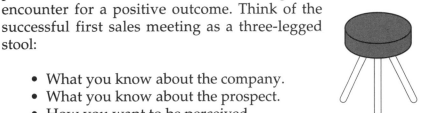

- What you know about the company.
- What you know about the prospect.
- How you want to be perceived.

Leg 1: What You Know About the Company

The more you know about the company you are calling on, its history, current challenges, competitors, and opportunities, the more comfortable the prospect will be with you—and impressed by your willingness to do a little homework on his behalf.

The purpose of arming yourself with homework is to help you avoid saying something dumb or making unwarranted assumptions about your prospect's business. It is not to

> **KYSO TIP:**
> Most prospects, once they meet you and feel comfortable with you, want to spend some time telling you all about their company and where it is headed. Let them. It is a very positive sign. Don't try and sound so smart that they don't get to tell you their story. (Take notes and ask good questions.)

make you seem like the smartest person in the room. That's the *prospect's* role.

If you are going to make a presentation on widget pickling equipment to ABC Widgets, you should, at least, know:

1. Whose equipment ABC is using now.

2. Why ABC is looking at new equipment. No one contemplates changing equipment or service vendors just for the heck of it. You need to know that reason so you can present your product or service as a solution to the problem the prospect has to solve. Possibilities to be on the lookout for:

   ✔ A big new customer.

   ✔ Equipment performance problems.

   ✔ Looking to reduce cost.

   ✔ Looking to improve quality.

   ✔ Equipment out of date.

3. What ABC's competitive position—and strategy—in the marketplace seems to be. Possibilities:

   ✔ Market leader   ✔ New entrant

   ✔ Niche player   ✔ Innovator

   ✔ Low price alternative   ✔ Oldest provider

Leg 2: Things to Know About the Prospect As a Person

The more you know about the prospect, the better you can shape the meeting to his or her comfort and style. Never hold a first sales meeting without knowing something about the prospect. A clueless first sales meeting is invariably worse than the worst blind date you've ever been on. Odds are, however, you've had at least a preliminary phone conversation with the prospect. If, for some reason, you've never spoken to the prospect, have gathered none of the information we suggested in a previous section, and know no one who knows the prospect, all is not yet lost. If the prospect has an assistant or secretary, call and plead your case: "Ms./Mr. Assistant, I have a meeting with Mr. Smith on Wednesday. He has asked me to present information on our approach to widget pickling and storage equipment. I'd like to make sure I use his time effectively. Would it be all right if I asked you a few questions to help me prepare?" Seven times out of ten the assistant or secretary is flattered by the request and indeed will give you a helping hand.

Things to Know About the Prospect

1. Name, title, department location, phone number, and e-mail address.
2. A thumbnail sketch of why you are meeting with the prospect.

    - If the prospect contacted you, what was he or she asking to hear about?
    - If you contacted the prospect, what about your initial chat seemed to interest him or her enough to schedule a meeting?

3. The prospect's personal communications style:$subItDid the prospect seem a serious person?

    - Time pressed?
    - A talkative person?
    - Interested in technical specifics or more relationship oriented?

    The odds are that someone in your company has called on this prospect before. Pump him or her about the things he or she remembers about ABC Widgets and Mr. Smith.
    The more you know about a prospect and his or her company, the less likely you are to make an embarrassing mistake.

Caution: Don't go overboard trying to "read" or "psychoanalyze" your prospect. You are just trying to learn enough about the person to make a good first impression and avoid obvious missteps.

Leg 3: The "You" You Want to Present

Cross-examine fifty salespeople and it's a good bet that not one of them will tell you they ever went in front of a prospect consciously planning to come across as a big-mouth braggart. It just "happens." It is also a good bet that very few of those fifty salespeople have ever written down exactly how they want a customer to see them or tried to figure out how to make that happen.

Try it.

On your last sales call, was your plan to be seen as:

- A good listener?
- A deal maker?
- A good person to play golf with?

- A product expert?
- A customer advocate?
- A likely social contact?

There are a lot of ways to decide how you want to be seen and dozens of factors to consider. The key is to decide.

Visualizing the kind of personal impact, the impression, you want to make is important. Another old axiom: "If you can't see it, you can't be it." So sit yourself down and decide: What impression do you want your first sales meetings with a customer to have? What are your strengths? What do existing customers say they appreciate most about you? What do friends say your good points are?

In fact, you may, at various times, be all sorts of different things to a customer during a long and productive relationship: problem solver, wise counselor, friend, advocate. But we are concerned here only with the impression you make in the crucial first meeting. Which *you* do you want your customer to perceive you to be at the first sales meeting?

Crime stopper's hint: Let's say your first sales meeting goes super well. And Mr. Smith calls back to tell you that the next step is to make your presentation all over again to a group, team, or committee. *Do not* yield to the temptation to see this as a second meeting. It is, in fact, a brand new "first sales meeting" with a team that Mr. Smith just happens to be a part of. You are right back at square one—Ok—square 2 maybe—in your preparations. Make sure you use Mr. Smith as an informant to help you prepare for the presentation. Nine times out of ten, Smith will simply tell you, "Oh Charlie, just make the same presentation you made to me. That'll be fine." Don't believe it, not for a minute! Follow up with a good second-order question: "Thank you for your confidence in my presentation. I'd like to be really sure I'm putting my best foot forward with your team. Could you take a minute and brief me on the people on your team and how each of them might be looking at the issue of purchasing new pickling equipment?" The odds here also are nine times out of ten that Mr. Smith will give you some helpful information.

Long-Term Success Is Always in the Details

Always leave time in your meeting planning to proofread materials, get help on graphics, and—in general—making 100% positive there are no embarrassing mistakes in your presentation materials. And that you arrive on time. And at the right place. With everything you promised to have with you in hand.

Business consultant Tom Peters put it well: "When the little flip down tray on the seat in front of you on the airplane is dirty and rickety, you begin to wonder about the quality of the airline's engine maintenance. It's not reasonable or rational. It's just the way customers are."

When your presentation materials are flawed, when your presentation is fraught with factual mistakes, when you look unprepared, anxious, and uncomfortable, the prospect begins to wonder about your ability to deliver on your product or service promises.

21

Moment of Truth Three:

Account Activation

The day the cable service is turned on, the new car is delivered, or the new grill is ignited is a memorable day—a day of anticipation, expectations, and focused attention. If the fire flares, the car hums and rides like a cloud, and the picture on the TV is clear and sharp, the customer is happy as a clam. If the cable is fuzzy, the fire fizzles, and the car is a flop, the customer tells everyone who will listen how horrible the cable company is, how unreliable the grill, and how bad the auto dealership.

You as the salesperson have no control over your company's product quality, when the new product model will be ready, or how the installation process goes. The customer doesn't care. And if everything doesn't work just the way you promised it would, the customer wants to know what you are going to do about it. To the customer *you* are the company.

So, you have no control of the delivery of the car, the switching on of the cable service, or the customer's first experience with the new grill. Too bad. That doesn't keep the customer from holding the problems or disappointments against you—and taking it out on you when there is another buying opportunity. And being on vacation or home with a cold doesn't help. The customer expects you to know how things went or at least be

159

available if they don't go well. So the question to ask yourself is:

How can I be a positive part of account activation?

Some Helpful Hints

- At Saturn dealerships, salespeople make a ceremony of turning the keys over to the buyers and congratulating them on their purchase. They are on the spot for every product delivery. Period. Make delivery memorable.
- Certain office furniture manufacturers make it a rule that the salesperson be present for the installation of a large order to reassure the customer and solve any problems. Just being there to say, "Yes, that's the way it's done. It will look just the way we planned it when they've finished" can short circuit a customer's installation-day anxieties.
- At Andersen Renewal, the window repair, replacement, and refurbishing arm of Andersen Windows Corp., salespeople call or visit homeowners at the end of the first day of an installation to ensure that both the outcome and the process of the work is satisfactory to the customer. They also do a detailed "walk through" of the premises with the homeowner at the end of the job to ensure that every detail from installation to premise clean-up meets the customer's expectations.

For some products and services, figuring out how to be a part of the account activation or installation process is a no brainer. You are a part of the process. Just "showing up" when the first shipment is delivered or the service is started is easy to arrange. In other situations you may be miles away. Being at the customer's site (or home) is too expensive or logistically impractical. Ok—but you still can get on the telephone and ask "How are things going?" while the work is in progress.

Say you are selling cable television. You only dealt with the customer over the phone—or at best he or she came to your office. Call the customer the day the installer is due. Ask how things are going. Extend an invitation to the customer to call you if the installer isn't there in the next ninety minutes. Reinforce the sale: "Mrs. Smith, I know that as soon as Roger gets you hooked up, you are really going to enjoy the wonderful difference cable makes. You don't hesitate to call me if you have any questions."

Seem like a lot of bother for a $30 to $50 a month sale? A study done in the cable TV industry a few years ago found that "account churn" makes a high percentage of sales unprofitable. That is, a high percentage of people who sign up for cable service don't stay long enough for the cost of sales, marketing, and installation to be offset by the customer's monthly payments. At the same time, customers report a little personal attention—early in the account life—does a lot to keep them customers for the long haul.

22

Moment of Truth Four:

The First Statement Arrives

So how big a deal can the arrival of the bill or first statement be? If you've ever tried to untangle a modern phone bill, make sense of a hospital statement, or closed on a house, you know *exactly* how offputting, upsetting, and just plain frightening a moment of truth this can be. Seeing the actual dollars of what you owe, right there in black and white, can be traumatic.

If you've done a good job up front of explaining the actual cost of your product or service, the shock will be minimized. Unfortunately, too many salespeople shy away from straight talk about the actual cost of things. Take the initiative. Build a smooth, accurate, and honest presentation around the real cost of your product or service. It shows confidence in the value of what you are selling.

Hint: When presenting dollars and cents to a prospect, talk about the cost in terms of the investment that is being made. Insurance is an investment in a family's *security*. Cable service is an investment in a family's *enjoyment*. A new car is an investment in trouble-free *transportation* and a sign of success (depending on the car). If you are selling to corporations rather than individuals and the negotiations for the exact features and benefits has been a long one and the price of some of the items has changed during the course of the sale, it is well worth your while to hand deliver the first statement and review the items on the statement and demonstrate how they fit within the terms of the contract.

As we said earlier, it demonstrates your confidence in the value of your product or service.

If the price of your product or simply geography prohibits your hand delivering the first statement or bill, it is a very good idea to carefully preview the costs of your product or service in writing after you have made the sale, or even when you are making the sale, although this can detract from your presentation and closing. One way to effectively preview the statement is to write out a brief case or example to work through with the customer. At the very least you need to invite the customer to contact you with questions when the statements start arriving.

If the idea of going over a statement with a customer doesn't thrill you—you aren't alone. Most salespeople see this as an invitation to injury. And if you are only planning on a single sale to this person or company, you can duck the responsibility of this moment of truth. But if you are looking forward to having this customer for a long, long time, then buckle up. This is the perfect opportunity to show that you are in deed, not just in words, interested in a long-term relationship with the customer.

23

Moment of Truth Five:

Post Sales Follow-Up

Remember the quote by Harvard professor Ted Levitt that opened this part?

> *"In the past, the relationship ended when the sale was made. To today's customer, the relationship begins when the sale is made."*

Levitt goes on to assert that today's customer thinks of your relationship as a marriage, rather than a date. Is that true of every customer—that they see you and your company as partners in an endeavor of long-term importance to both of you? No. Certainly not. Many customers do indeed want to keep their suppliers and vendors at arm's length.

But many more customers, particularly in business-to-business situations, expect you to follow up, keep in touch, and become a part of the fabric of his or her operation. Some customers fully expect you to act like a partner in their business—someone vitally interested in their long-term success. And if you are supplying a product or service to customers with these expectations, it behooves you to start thinking like a partner.

How Partners Differ from Customers

We asked major players in ten companies who say they believe in partnering with their vendors and suppliers—and their customers—to tell us how partnership differs from customership. This is what they told us:

Customers/End Users	Partners
• Buy on price, rather than performance or service.	• Have more realistic expectations—learn from dialogue with you.
• Switch on errors or just whim.	• Forgiving of errors—as long as your recovery is top rate.
• Have roving eyes. Are always looking for a "better deal."	• Give you feedback—ample feedback. In fact, feel free to tell you exactly how to change your business practices.
• Don't feel obliged to share disquiet or upset—or anything else—with you.	• Champion you in the marketplace. Brag about being your customer.

Who Qualifies for Partnership

How do you know who is a good candidate for partnership? Dr. Chip Bell, author of *Customers as Partners*, advises that three conditions should exist before considering a move toward a partnered relationship with a customer. Specifically, both parties:

1. **Should be interested.** Partnerships are mutually beneficial and need to be mutually desirable. They require too much commitment and hard work to be entered into frivolously.

2. **Willing to take risks.** Partners try new things together, explore mutual opportunities, and occasionally fail together. Key point. Partners attack the marketplace together. They both succeed or they both fail together.

3. **Willing to forgo profit now for future gain.** Partners look out for each other. Your customer/partner must be willing to take less from time to time, and so must you be.

Successful customer partnerships are possible and the results can be real. But these new combinations require a lot of time and effort to succeed. They require a degree of openness and shared risk that few companies are comfortable extending to one another. Much of the "how-to-succeed" advice from people studying partnerships sounds as if it comes from a marriage manual:

- Don't take the relationship for granted.
- Listen to the other partner and respect their views even if you disagree.
- Communicate a lot.

- Share fears and feelings.
- Don't be afraid to say I'm sorry or ask for feedback.
- Practice forgiveness.
- Consider conflict as a sign of a healthy growing relationship.
- Celebrate successes and learn from failures.

The list is potentially endless, but the advice sage, whether applied to a marriage or a strategic partnership.

The key of keys, says research Jordan Lewis, is trust: "Success of an alliance depends on mutual faith. It's hard to take risks with someone you don't trust."

Think Like a Partner

Even if your organization isn't exploring formal customer partnerships, you can adopt a partnership mindset with your customers.

24

Moment of Truth Six:

Communicating During the "Doldrums"

"Out of sight, out of mind" is the key to this moment of truth. If the only time the customer sees or hears from you is when you need an order or the contract is up for renewal, don't be surprised if the greeting you receive is a cool one. Today's customer expects to hear from his or her vendors and suppliers on a regular basis. And they expect that contact to be more than social. In fact, in today's high-pressure, time-sensitive marketplace, calling a customer just to "chit chat" is a net negative. The key is to make those contacts between sales opportunities value-adding, relationship-building occasions.

As we pointed out earlier, customers evaluate your company on two criteria:

1. The quality and value of your products and services, and
2. How "easy to do business with" you are.

Long-term relationship building means making sure your company continues to be seen as "easy to do business with" and as adding value to the business relationship through you.

How do you do that? Here are starter suggestions for both categories.

- Plan a regular review of account activity and problems. Set up a regular schedule to hold this review. A sequence we like is:
  - End of the first week
  - End of the first month
  - End of the first full quarter
  - Quarterly thereafter

- Invite customers to in-house educational events. Involve them in customer panels and new product idea reviews. Track who has been invited to what, so that every customer is tapped for some special event at least three times a year.
- When people in your company are asked to make association presentations, make it a policy to invite customers to be a part of the presentation.
- Hold user conferences at least twice a year. Invite customers to come and exchange ideas and problems with other customers.
- Involve customers in new product or product upgrade tests. Asking a customer to try your version "3.3 Next" software or widget is flattering—and it gives you useful information.
- Hire a clipping service to track published information about your company and your customers. When flattering stories about the customer organizations show up, laminate them and send them off to the customer.
- Any time you read an article in a trade journal that pertains to the widget industry or something you know the customer has an interest in, clip or copy it, add a handwritten "thought you might find this interesting," and send it off.

The Newsletter Option

Newsletters, print or electronic, are more popular today than full-blown business journals. These days, most people don't have time for long stories and articles. If your company has a newsletter, be sure it goes to all your customers. If you don't have a company newsletter or are an independent representative, consider starting one.

Newsletters tell news through stories. Let the stories be told through your customers. Make them the heroes. You can still tell stuff about your people (and if you're adamant about telling everything about all your employees to every other employee—make two separate newsletters).

Here are suggested newsletter components. Not all have to be in every newsletter, but the common thread is customers and photographs:

- Big headline about the customer with their name.
- Tell stories about happy endings that make the customer the hero.
- Talk about partnership strategies.
- Tell stories about industry trends and how they affect customers, and how others are using our products (nearby or far away).

- Welcome new customers!
- Feature story about the success of a customer using your product.
- Feature story about our employees and how they serve customers, the community, and their family.
- Tell stories of employee achievement (ours and theirs).
- Feature story about product application in a customer's place of business (it's more important to know how your product is used than how your product is sold).
- Feature story about a new product at a customer location.
- Feature story about heroic customer service.
- Lots of photographs of customers, customers, customers.
- Lots of photographs of employees and customers working together.
- Show the golf tournament, the trade shows, the seminars. Events where customers interact with employees.
- Get personal about the philosophy of selling, serving, and success.
- Show how your partnerships are working.

One absolute: The newsletter is an example of your company's quality. It's not just news—it's your image. It must be professionally designed and printed on high-quality paper by an experienced, first-class commercial printer.

After the newsletters are printed, get them into the marketplace quickly. Lots of them. Here's the distribution list:

- Your customers
- Your prospects
- Your vendors, and
- Major people of the community or industry influence.

Take at least an extra hundred copies to each featured customer (or whatever quantity they want—they may want to mail it to all of their customers).

Frame one copy for every customer featured. When you deliver the stack of newsletters you want them to mail to their customers, remain in their lobby, and give the newsletters to their employees (especially the ones with the photos of them in it), you will surprise and delight them. It will be hung in a place of honor.

Here are a few more things to think about:

- Think the customer will show the story around the town? A hundred times? You bet.
- Think those photographs will be reshown by the people in them? A hundred times? You bet.
- Think the customer's loyalty to your company grows? A hundred times? You bet.
- How do you think your competition will feel when he calls on your customer and sees your newsletter framed in their lobby with a bunch of happy people and a big headline? A bit deflated? You bet.
- Think you may get a few unsolicited referrals from the gesture and the publicity? You bet.

Net-net: The newsletter is a vehicle to increase sales, build customer loyalty, eliminate competition, and get more referrals. It sounds like a sure thing. Almost. Last piece of advice—do it before your competition does.

25

Moment of Truth Seven:

Problem Solving

Things don't always work out right. They should, but they don't. When they go wrong, it's time to play your trump card:

"Knock Your Socks Off Problem Solving."

Here's a true fact:

- Customers who have had a problem with your company and have seen it solved faster, better, and easier than they expected are 20 percent more loyal than problem-free customers.

There are two more important, related facts:

- Customers expect their salesperson to know the problems they are having with the company, and
- Customers expect their salesperson to take a hand in solving their problems—when asked.

Based on these facts, we suggest five rules for being seen as Knock Your Socks Off Problem Solvers:

Rule 1: Be Aware

Never go into a meeting with a customer without checking to see if there have been any performance problems or other account glitches since your last meeting or without complete knowledge of how those problems were resolved.

Walking into a customer's office not knowing that there have been problems—be they quality, service, delivery, billing, whatever—sends a negative message to your customer. It says, "I don't care enough to keep up with what's happening to your business." It also ends whatever business you had planned on pursuing with the customer. Conversely, knowing the problems and their status gives you an opportunity to summarize what has gone on, then move to new business.

Rule 2: Investigate

Whenever you hear that there is a problem with an account—investigate. And do it immediately. Start internally, with whoever handles the account on a day-to-day basis and is likely to hear the customer's complaints. Once you have the inside story, follow up with the customer or the customer's key contact people. Find out if the customer is upset. Find out what the problem looks like from his or her perspective. In short, learn both sides of the "story."

Rule 3: Listen, Probe, and Follow Up

Listening. The importance of listening can't be overstated. Listening is important for two reasons:

- To allow your customer to vent his or her frustrations or irritation, and
- To find the real problem (which may be obvious, but sometimes isn't).

Listen to this retail level customer problem:

"I bought a Kid-Pro Bike from you people last night. The box must have weighed eighty pounds! I finally got it into my car—no help from you guys—and home, and it took me an hour to get it out of the car, into the house, and open. I mean really! This is a kid's bike and you need Arnold Schwarzenegger to open the box! And, after all that, the directions were missing! How am I supposed to put it together without the directions?!"

KYSO TIP:
Your customer has been practicing her little speech. Don't deprive her of the right to deliver it, and in as dramatic a fashion as she likes. Even if you are sure you understand the problem—don't interrupt. You may be right, but you may not be. Listen until your customer is done explaining. She'll feel better for getting the whole story off her chest, and you may discover pieces of the puzzle you didn't even know were missing.

Upset customers are apt to bring multiple issues into their tirade. It's important to this customer that she had difficulty leaving the store, getting the box from her car to the house, and opening the box. But the immediate problem is the missing directions.

Probing

Upset customers don't always explain things clearly, completely, or even rationally and accurately. The customer who says, "You people have screwed this up seventeen times this month," is probably engaging in hyperbole—and doesn't need to be reminded of the facts. Telling him, "Oh no, Mr. Smith. Our records indicate we've only screwed up three times," doesn't help.

But do ask questions about anything you may not understand or that you need clarified. "Mr. Smith, can you describe what exactly was off loaded on your dock this morning?" Then, when you have identified and clearly understand the problem, or at least the customer's view of the problem, repeat it back to make sure you have it right.

> *"I'm concerned about your experience with shipping and billing systems, and I'm going to look into what's going on as soon as I hang up. What you need right away is for us to move the overshipment off your receiving dock. Is that right? I've been on your dock and I can see how the extra pallets can be causing a traffic problem for you."*

Follow-Up

Going back to the customer with a solution—or simply to verify that the problem has been solved—pays dividends. It gives the customer a chance to create closure and you an opportunity to ensure that everything is back on track.

Additionally, if you've promised the customer some sort of action, you must get back to him or her to confirm that your promise will be, or is being, kept, and the details are clearly understood and under control.

Two More "Do"s and a "Don't Ever"

There are two more Knock Your Socks Off Problem Solving steps that will take you out of the realm of the mundane and into the class of super problem solver.

Rule 4: Apologize

The solution to every problem, whether major or minor, should start with a sincere apology. Our research shows that when customers tell a company about a problem with a product or service, they receive an apology less than half the time. That's about half as often as they should. Ironically, a sincere "I'm sorry for your inconvenience" does wonders for curing customer upsets.

Why is it so hard for us to say, "I'm sorry," to our customers? First and foremost, we may be intimidated by the words. We may think that "I'm sorry" says "I've failed," "I'm not a good person," or "I'm not professional." Nothing could be further from the truth. An apology is simply an acknowledgment that things aren't going right in your customer's eyes.

Today, there is also a tendency to equate being sorry with an admission of personal or corporate liability, an equation of being sorry with somehow being to blame. If your job has legal or regulatory aspects, make sure you understand what they are and how they affect what you do. But don't assume that you're not allowed to say, "I'm sorry you were inconvenienced" when a snafu occurs. Actually, a sincere apology, delivered in a timely and professional manner, often goes a long way toward heading off potential legal problems. When you show your willingness to make sure your customers receive what they expect to receive, you relieve them of the need to even think about starting a fight.

Do It Right

A vague apology delivered in an impersonal, machine-like manner can be worse than no apology at all. Effective apologies are:

1. **Sincere.** Although you may not know exactly what your customers are feeling and experiencing individually, you can be genuine in your concern.
2. **Personal.** Apologies are far more powerful when they are delivered in the first person: "I am sorry that you experiencing a problem." Remember that to the customer, you—not some mysterious we or they—are the company.
3. **Timely.** Don't wait to find out why there is a problem or what caused it before expressing regret that the problem exists in the first place. The sooner you react to a distressed customer, the better.

Rule 5: Practice Atonement

It's not uncommon for a dissatisfied customer to feel injured or put out by a breakdown. Often they will look to you to provide some value-added gesture—some recompense—that says, "I want to make it up to you."

Remember, beyond solving the problem it is vital to rebuild the relationship when something has gone wrong for a customer. Rebuilding a damaged relationship, particularly when a customer feels victimized by the problem, may require taking an extra step—something we call "symbolic atonement." It means making a gesture that says, "I want to make it up to you." Atonement is a way of providing a value-added touch that tells the customer his or her business is important to you:

> *"I'm glad you gave us this chance to make things right, Mr. Smith. I'm going to make sure we don't charge you for the first month's shipment. Let me give you my home phone and my pager number so you can contact me directly if anything should go wrong for you again."*

And the Final Rule: "Don't" Scapegoat (Call This Rule 5.5)

When things go wrong, there's an almost instinctive urge to direct the customer's attention elsewhere: "If those 'smart guys' in computer services could ever figure out how to make this billing system work the way it's supposed to, we wouldn't have to put you through an over ship like this," or "Logistics was supposed to have all the bugs out of the just-in-time system last month. They really owe us all an apology."

Scapegoating another part of your organization for a service breakdown simply tells your customers that you're separate departments working in isolated and even adversarial ways, instead of a tight-knit team working for them. Don't do it—not to each other and not to yourself.

Being an active player in solving customer problems is a key element in long-term customer relations. It makes your selling job easier. It's a tremendous way to mend an at-risk relationship and make a satisfied customer even more loyal.

Part Four

Knock Your Socks Off Selling Fitness:

Taking Care of You

We've focused our attention primarily on the customers and prospects. But there's another important player in the sales game: you. A savvy sales professional learns that self-management is every bit as important as managing the customer's experience.

Knock Your Socks Off Selling shouldn't be an impossible quest—or a personal ordeal. Like an athlete constantly in training

or a musician perfecting an instrument, you need to develop, evaluate, pace, and manage yourself as well as your perfor- mance. That means work, but it also means celebrating a job well done.

How you feel about yourself and the job you are doing— whether you love it or are overwhelmed by it—inevitably will be reflected in the quality of your work. Knock Your Socks Off Selling should be a joy, not a job.

26

Mastering the Art of Calm

You're not any good to anyone when you are stressed up, stressed out, overwrought, anxious, moody, belligerent, nasty, and still waiting for that first cup of coffee. The emotional labor involved in modern selling can actually be more draining than lifting boxes or pouring concrete. All the good stuff built into your job will never be enough if you don't learn how to cope with and counteract the stress of selling for a living.

The problem is that, in selling, you are out there, on stage all by yourself. You are more "exposed" than almost any other professional.

There is an *organizational* fix for some of the stress you experience that we learned from the theme-park industry.

At parks from Disneyland and Walt Disney World to Knott's Berry Farm, Opryland, and Carowinds, people at the frontlines are taught the concepts of *on stage* and *off stage*.

> *On stage* is anywhere a customer can see or hear you.
> *Off stage* is everywhere else, safely away from the public eye.

You, your manager, and your organization have to work together to manage the environment in which you work to make it a safe haven—off stage—for you and your colleagues. But only you can manage the way you react to a given service encounter. How do you cope? There are any number of techniques for reducing stress, whether inside your car or out on the sales floor.

Parts of this chapter are excerpted from "Delivering Knock Your Socks Off Service," 2nd Edition, AMACOM, 1998.

Find those that work best for you and practice them every day. Here are ten to get you started.

Ten Stress Reducers

1. **Breathe.** Deep breathing is one of the oldest stress-busting techniques, and one of the best. Stress can upset the normal balance of oxygen and carbon dioxide in your lungs. Deep breathing corrects this imbalance and can help you control panic thinking. Take a deep breath through your nose—hold it for seven seconds (no more)—then let it out slowly through your mouth. Do this three to six times.
2. **Smile.** You make your mood, and your mood can stress or relax you. Smiling is contagious. When you see a customer looking a little glum, make eye contact and turn on one of your best and brightest. Ninety-nine times out of a hundred, you'll get a smile right back.

3. **Laugh.** Maintaining a sense of humor is your best defense against stress. Stress psychologist Frances Meritt Stern tells of a difficult client she had been dealing with for years. "That clown is driving me up a wall!" she often complained. One day, she began to envision him complete with white-face, floppy shoes, and a wide, foolish grin. With this picture tickling her funny bone, she was able to manage her stress response and focus on doing her job.

4. **Let it out.** Keep your anger and frustration locked up inside and you are sure to show it on the outside to your customers. Instead, make an appointment with yourself to think about a particularly stressful customer later—and then keep the appointment. Unacknowledged tension will eat you up, but delaying your reaction to stress-causing events can be constructive. It puts you in control.

5. **Take a one-minute vacation.** John Rondell, a sales consultant, has a vivid image of himself snorkeling off a beautiful white-sand beach in the Caribbean. He has worked on the scene until he can experience being there and lose all sense of time and place, even though his visits last only a minute or two. Now he can return to his "favorite place" after a stressful call or before talking to a stress-inducing customer.

6. **Relax.** We tend to hold in tension by tightening our muscles. Instead, try isometrics: tensing and relaxing specific muscles or muscle groups. Make a fist, then relax it. Tighten your stomach muscles, then relax them. Push your palms against each other, then relax your arms. Some people get so good at it, they can do their exercises right under the customer's nose.

> **KYSO TIP:**
> When your customer is the most anxious, you need to be at your best—most competent, confident, calmest, and in control of yourself.

7. **Do desk aerobics.** Exercise is a vital component of a stress-managed life. Try these two "desk-ercises":

- While sitting at your desk, raise your feet until your legs are almost parallel to the floor. Hold them there, then let them down. Do this five times.
- Rotate your head forward and from side to side (but not back—that can strain rather than stretch). Roll your shoulders forward and then lift them up and back. This feels especially good after you've been sitting or standing for some time.

8. **Organize.** Organizing gives you a sense of control and lessens your stress level. "I organize the top of my desk whenever I am waiting on hold," says Amin Johnson, a telephone sales representative. "Before I leave for the day, I make sure everything is put away and that I have a list of priorities made out for the next day."

9. **Talk positively.** Vent your anger and frustration in positive ways. Sharing customer encounters with coworkers helps you find the humor in the situation and gain new ideas for handling similar situations. But constant negative talk that rehashes old ground will only recreate and reinforce, not diminish, your stress.

10. **Take a health break.** Make your normal breaks into stress breaks. Consider walking outside, reading a chapter from a favorite book, or just sitting with your eyes closed for a few minutes. Bring healthy snacks and juice to work to substitute for the standard coffee and donuts.

To paraphrase: You can only sell as good as you feel. You need to take care of yourself. And you are the only one who can.

27

Becoming a Lifelong Learner

You can only grow when you know. The half-life of the knowledge of this year's graduating MIT engineer is three to five years. That means half of everything that engineer knows will be out of date in less time than it took to earn the degree. For salespeople, out there on the frontline, on the tip of the surfboard riding the shock wave of change, it is obvious that keeping up is a lifetime assignment and challenge.

Here are 12.5 ideas the lifelong learning sales professionals we know endorse wholeheartedly.

Rate yourself in the box on the left of each of these lifelong learning strategies.

(1 = poor;   2 = average;   3 = good;   4 = very good;   5 = the greatest)

or

(1 = never;   2 = rarely;   3 = sometimes;   4 = frequently;   5 = always).

❏   1. *Learn how to achieve a positive attitude.* Gather the information of the world's most positive people in your library.

Napoleon Hill	Dale Carnegie	W. Clement Stone
Maxwell Maltz	Wayne Dyer	Earl Nightingale
Norman Vincent Peale		Jim Rohn

Every time you read something written by one of these or other gurus of positive attitude you should come away—at a minimum—with ten note cards of wisdom that you review on a regular basis. At least monthly.

❑   2. *Listen to audio tapes.* Own several sets and play them in your car. Swap tapes with other salespeople. Discuss them. Again, write down the best ideas and keep them in your 3" x 5" card pack.

❑   3. *Read books.* Build your library. Read one book a month. Again, make notes. Review the notes. Discuss what you learned with anyone you can. Own the information by sharing it with others.

❑   4. *Attend live seminars.* Attend as many as you can afford— as often as you can. Take notes, sure, but more than anything else, absorb the emotion and positive atmosphere. One selling seminar can recharge your mental batteries for months.

❑   5. *Join Toastmasters.* Ninety minutes of speaking and self-evaluation a week. Use Toastmasters for contacts, sure. But do the work called for and you will improve. Take it seriously. It is a tremendous discipline.

❑   6. *Record yourself speaking—a weekly ritual.* Practice your presentation or rehearse your answers to objections. If you sell over the phone, record and critique your calls. Save the super good ones. Use them as reminders and models of how good you can be.

❑   7. *Record yourself reading—a weekly ritual.* Reading aloud gives you an opportunity to practice vocal control, pacing, and emphasis without having to also think up the words.

❑   8. *Record yourself selling—a weekly ritual.* If you sell or prospect over the phone, this won't be a problem. Devices for connecting a cassette recorder to your phone cost pennies. Recording a face-to-face presentation requires a lot of trust on the part of the prospect.

❑   9. *Record your personal commercial—a weekly ritual.* Your thirty-second commercial is a precious commodity. Practice it, revise it, use it. Rule of thumb: You should practice your thirty-second commercial for thirty minutes once a week.

❑   10. *Record your own set of sales tapes—get great at selling and presenting at the same time.* It costs a couple of dollars to edit together the "best of you" from all the sales presentations you've made and recorded. But your own personal highlight reel is a priceless personal pep talk starring you.

❑   11. *Listen to your own tapes as much as you listen to others.* Really. Don't be shy. When you are in the heat of battle it's hard to remember what you did or said that impressed—or annoyed—the prospect, but the evidence is right there—on tape.

❑   12. *Spend thirty minutes a day learning something new.* This doesn't have to be just something about selling on your products. It can be juggling or locksmithing. The key is to stay flexible and focused—to be a learning vacuum cleaner.

❑   12.5 *Practice what you've learned as soon as you learn it.* The learning's not over until it leads to new behavior. Don't stop with knowledge. Make a plan for putting every new idea into action at least once.

Score: 65–70 = WOW!   59–64 = AOK
           40–59 = Get Help!   20–40 = Start Over

28

The Post-It™ Notes Goal-Setting Method

Industrial psychologist David Campbell says it well: "If you don't know where you're going, any road will get you there." Without goals you never know where you are or how you are doing—and you certainly never know when you've gotten there.

Goals are the road map to success. Everyone knows that, but fewer that 5 percent of people in our society sets and achieves them.

Goals are related to everything we strive to achieve, from our daily to-do list to earning a million dollars.

Goal setting and goal achievement is a science and a self-discipline that must be practiced every day. How do you set and achieve your goals? Here's a method that works well.

A pad of Post-It™ notes can put you on the path to greater achievement!

Follow this formula:

- **Write down the big ones.** On 3" x 3" yellow Post-It™ notes, write down your three prime goals in short phrases with bold letters (get $25,000 funding for business; new car—Beamer; new client—NationsBank).
- **Write down the small ones.** Write down your three secondary goals in short phrases with bold letters (read book—Dale Carnegie; organize desk; build new closet).

188

- **Post them**. Put the Post-It™ goals on your bathroom mirror where you can see them twice each day—you are forced to look at them every morning and evening.
- **Keep looking and reading them aloud until you act.** You will look at them twice every day. You will read them aloud twice a day. You will look at them and read them until you are sick of looking at them and reading them—and then you will begin to accomplish them. By posting the goal in the bathroom you are consciously reminded of your goals several times a day. From there your subconscious gets into the act—gnawing away at your inner soul until you are driven to take positive action. Achievement action. Keep at it until:

At last you can say the magic words—scream them—I DID IT!

(Screaming positive things always feels wonderful.)

Start your day by looking at your success—after your goal is achieved. Take it off the bathroom mirror and triumphantly post it on your bedroom mirror so you can see your success every time you look in that mirror. Not only does it feel great, but you get to set the tone for a successful day, every day, first thing in the morning. Plus, it gets you motivated to keep achieving more.

The program is simple. The program works. The results will change your attitude. The results will change your outlook about your capability to achieve success. The results will change your life.

We urge you to give this process a solid thirty-day trial. Use more small goals than big goals at first, so you can get immediate gratification. Post it. Post haste.

29

The Knock Your Socks Off Selling Checkup

We began this book with a series of assessments. We asked you to decide whether Knock Your Socks Off Selling was really for you—and to frankly assess your current level of skill. Along the way we've added a lot of nuances to the things you need to know—and be able to do—if you are going to succeed in Knock Your Socks Off Selling. What follows is the "mother of all assessments." We call it the "101.5 Rules for Selling Success" assessment.

These "rules," gleaned from every chapter and crack and crevice in this book, cover the gamut. The checklist is designed to be your annual sales checkup. You have a physical regularly, don't you? You need a professional selling checkup annually as well.

These rules are designed to remind you of the gaps of skill that still might exist and to reinforce your progress toward perfection. You can gain maximum benefit from this annual challenge if you follow these three steps:

1. Evaluate yourself on each item. In the box next to the item rate yourself on a 1 to 5 scale:

   1 = I do this poorly *or* never do it.

   5 = I do this well *or* all the time.

   2. If you rate yourself between good and poor on any item, if you rate yourself 1-2-3-4, make an action plan for improvement.

   3. Do it. NOW!

❑   1. *Develop and maintain a positive attitude.* The first rule of life. The way you think is the way you behave and achieve. Your sales (and life's) success depend on it.

❑   2. *Believe in yourself first.* If you don't think you can do it, who will?

❑   3. *Set and achieve goals.* Make a plan. A goal is a dream with a plan behind it.

❑   4. *Learn and execute the fundamentals of sales.* Never stop learning how to sell. Read, listen to tapes, attend seminars. Concentrate on the fundamentals. Adapt sales techniques to your own style and personality.

❑   5. *Learn one new technique a day.* Practice the new technique at least twice as soon as you learn it.

❑   6. *Use your car as a learning center.* A sales tape is better for your success than talk radio or classic rock.

❑   7. *Visualize the sale taking place before it actually happens.* You'll become assumptive and confident, and you'll double your sales.

❑   8. *Sell on your home court as often as possible.* Seventy-five percent of professional sports team win their home games. That's a great winning percentage. Try it.

❑   9. *Shake hands firmly.* No one wants to shake hands with a dead fish. It's a little thing that makes a big impact.

❑   10. *Be conversational in your presentation.* Give your presentation as though you were talking to friends. Be original in the way you present. Make your self memorable—in a positive way.

❑   11. *Develop great telephone skills.* The most deadly weapon in sales.

❑   12. *Never prejudge prospects.* They are often customers in the disguise of a doubter.

❑   13. *Understand the customer and meet his or her needs.* Question and listen to the prospect and uncover true needs. The skill of questioning is at the heart of understanding.

❑   14. *Qualify the buyer.* Don't waste time with someone who can't decide. It's a hard but critical rule. Presentations to nondecision makers lead to nonsales—and nothing more.

❑   15. *Develop a test to see if you can help (hook the prospect).* Build ten questions that will qualify and interest the prospect at the same time.

❑   16. *Take notes as the prospect or customer is talking.* It makes him or her feel important and captures the information to help make the sale.

❑   17. *Listen with the intent to understand.* When you feel you understand, then respond. Listening is more important than talking.

❑   18. *Communicate to be understood.* Be clear, concise, brief, and memorable.

❑   19. *Sell to help.* Sell to help customers; don't sell for commissions. The dollars follow when the help is there.

❑ 20. *Establish long-term relationships with everyone.* If you get to know your customer and concentrate on his best interests, you'll earn much more than a commission.

❑ 21. *Believe in your company and product.* Believe your product or service is the best and it will show. If you don't believe in your product, your prospect won't either. Be loyal to your company and product or quit.

❑ 22. *Be prepared.* Your self-motivation and preparation are the lifeblood of your outreach. Be ready to make the sale with sales kit, sales tools, openers, questions, statements, and answers.

❑ 23. *Know the prospect's industry.* Do your homework before you make the call.

❑ 24. *Know the prospect's business.* Do your homework before you make the call.

❑ 25. *Know the prospect.* Do your homework before you make the call.

❑ 26. *Understand how your prospect serves his or her customer.* You must understand how your prospect's business or customer uses your product.

❑ 27. *Read the trade journals of your best customers.* Know what's going on in their world.

❑ 28. *Get the prospect to lean forward.* Gain buyer interest or you'll never get a sale. You may not even get an appointment. Your creative preparation will determine your outcome.

❑ 29. *Become a resource to your customers.* Ideas, industry information, and competitive information make you a resource. Go to a sales call with an idea you think your prospect can use.

❑ 30. *Be sincere.* If you are sincere about helping, it w
show—and vice versa.

❑ 31. *Be on time for everything.* Lateness says you don't respect
their time. There is no excuse for lateness—or for disre-
spect.

❑ 32. *Look professional.* If you look sharp, it's a positive reflec-
tion on you, your company, and your product. Tangi-
bles count.

❑ 33. *Establish rapport and confidence before selling.* Get to know
the prospect and his company; establish confidence
early. Don't start your pitch until you do.

❑ 34. *Use humor.* It's the best tool for relationship sales. Have
fun at what you do. Laughing is tacit approval. Make
the prospect laugh.

❑ 35. *Be a master of your product.* Know how your product is
used to benefit your customers. Total product knowledge gives you the mental freedom to concentrate on
selling. You may not always use the knowledge in the
sales presentation, but it gives you confidence to make
the sale. Become an expert in your industry.

❑ 36. *The power of the question cannot be equaled.* You can qualify the buyer, establish rapport, create disparity, eliminate competition, build credibility, know the customer,
identify needs, find hot buttons, get personal information, and close a sale—all by asking questions. Have
twenty-five of the most powerful ones you can create—
at your fingertips.

❑ 37. *Questions.* Create a buying atmosphere—not a selling
one.

38. *Sell solutions (benefits), not situations (features).* The customer doesn't want to know how it works. He wants to know how it will help him.

❑ 39. *Tell the truth.* Never be at a loss to remember what you said.

❑ 40. *Deliver on all promises.* The best way to turn a sale into a relationship is to deliver as promised. Failure to do what you say you're going to do for either your company or your customer is a disaster from which you may never recover.

❑ 41. *Never put down the competition.* If you have nothing nice to say, say nothing. Set yourself apart from them with preparation and creativity—don't put them down.

❑ 42. *Use testimonials.* The strongest salesman on your team is a reference from a satisfied customer. Testimonials are proof positive.

❑ 43. *Use testimonials to overcome objections.* Get from satisfied customers letters that overcome standard objections.

❑ 44. *Learn to recognize buying signals.* The prospect often will tell you when he is ready to buy—if you're paying attention.

❑ 45. *The biggest buying signal in the world is "How much is it?"* Don't tell the price until the prospect asks. The price question says, "I like it—can I afford it?"

❑ 46. *Objections often indicate buyer interest.* When the buyer objects, it often means he wants to buy—with contingencies. It definitely means he is paying attention.

❑ 47. *Anticipate objections.* There are always fewer than ten objections to your sale. Have answers to all of the common ones written out. Rehearse answers to standard objections.

❏ 48. *Get down to the real objection.* Customers are not always truthful; they often won't tell you the true objection(s) at first. Sometimes it's embarrassing to admit the actual objection.

❏ 49. *Know the difference between a stall and an objection.* Excuses like "I want to think it over" are not objections.

❏ 50. *Incorporate answers to objections into your presentation.* Don't wait for them to be raised.

❏ 51. *Overcome objections.* This is a complex issue. An "overcome" is not just an answer, it's an understanding of the situation. Listen to the prospect and think in terms of a solution. You must create an atmosphere of confidence and trust strong enough to effect a sale.

❏ 52. *Create a comparison chart of all your competitors for the buyer who wants to "shop around."* Lead into it with, "Mr. Johnson, after you shop, if you find we're the best, will you select us?" Then show the chart and write up the order.

❏ 53. *Close the sale.* Use the same words the prospect gave you when he was answering his "biggest need" question.

❏ 54. *Ask for the sale.* Sounds too simple, but it works, and it isn't done nearly enough.

❏ 55. *Once you ask a closing question, shut up!* The first rule of sales.

❏ 56. *If you don't make the sale, make a firm appointment to return.* Make some form of sale each time you call.

❏ 57. *Follow up, follow up, follow up.* If it takes between five and ten exposures to a prospect before a sale is made, be prepared to do whatever it takes to get to the tenth meeting.

❑   58. *Redefine rejection.* They're not rejecting you, they're just rejecting the offer you're making them.

❑   59. *Anticipate and be comfortable with change.* A big part of sales is change. Roll with it to succeed. Fight it and fail.

❑   60. *Follow rules.* Salespeople often think rules are made for others. Think again. Broken rules will only get you fired by your customers.

❑   61. *Team up with coworkers.* Work internally as a team to serve the customer in the best way possible. Sales is never a solo effort. Team up with your coworkers so you can partner with your customers.

❑   62. *Never argue.* Never argue. Never argue with a prospect or a customer. Even if you win, you lose.

❑   63. *Negative emotions inhibit sales.* They block clear creative thinking.

❑   64. *Deliver more than expected* the day before it's due.

❑   65. *Surprise your customers,* so they'll talk about you to someone else.

❑   66. *Treat every customer as though he or she were the king or queen of England or some imagined celebrity.* Deference and respect are impressive. They also are rare.

❑   67. *Treat others the way you want to be treated.* Provide the same service you expect to get. Put yourself in the other person's shoes. Do they fit?

❑   68. *Satisfy a customer's complaint in less than twenty-four hours.* Positive recovery leads to more sales and a great reputation.

❑   69. *Never blame others when the fault (or responsibility) is yours.*
         Take full responsibility for your actions, what happens
         to you, and the success of your company. Accepting re-
         sponsibility is the fulcrum point for succeeding at any-
         thing. Doing something about it is the criterion. Blame
         yourself for lost sales.

❑   70. *Understand that hard work makes luck.* Take a close look at
         the people you think are lucky. Either they or someone
         in their family put in years of hard work to create that
         luck. You can get just as lucky. Success and failure are
         not accidents or luck driven.

❑   71. *Harness the power of persistence.* Are you willing to take
         no for an answer and just accept it without fight? Can
         you take no as a challenge instead of a rejection? Are
         you willing to resist through the five to ten exposures it
         takes to make the sale? Be as tenacious and persistent as
         you were when you were four years old and asked your
         mom for a candy bar in the supermarket.

❑   72. *Find your success formula through numbers.* Determine
         your own numbers for success—how many leads, calls,
         proposals, appointments, presentations, and follow-
         ups it takes to get to the sale. Then follow the formula.

❑   73. *Develop and practice networking skills.* The most powerful
         business tool in the twenty-first century.

❑   74. *Spend more than ten hours a month networking.* The only
         way to get results is to be there.

❑   75. *Develop a thirty-second personal commercial that generates
         interest in your product or service.* Practice it until it's per-
         fect.

❑   76. *Write on the back of business cards.* This is the best way to
         capture important information while networking.

❑ 77. *Design and invest in a great business card.* It's your image after you leave. Have a business card that people talk about.

❑ 78. *Take advantage of every second of your time.* It's all you've got.

❑ 79. *Schedule a sales call one minute after your sales meeting.* Try out what you just learned.

❑ 80. *Implement the daily-dose formula.* Reduce what it takes to succeed to a daily dose. Do that amount every day. The longest journey begins with a single step. Sounds simple? It is simple!

❑ 81. *Evaluate yourself every month.* Your presentation, your sales and personal goal achievement, your education, and your attitude.

❑ 82. *Do it down to the last detail.* Too often salespeople ignore details—and fail.

❑ 83. *Gain the ability to make effective decisions.* This means taking risks. Don't be afraid to be wrong—it inhibits growth.

❑ 84. *The two acid sales questions.* Is this in the best interest of my customers? Is this in the best long-term interest of my company? If yes, do it.

❑ 85. *Make it easy for anyone to do business with you.* Fill out the forms yourself. Be easy to do business with in every aspect of the sale.

❑ 86. *Do something nonbusiness with a customer.* A meal, ball game, or theater tickets help turn customers into business friends. People buy from friends.

❑ 87. *Get others business.* A powerful relationship builder and implied position of obligation. Your customers need customers just as you do.

❑ 88. *Don't keep score.* Use every resource at your disposal to help others. If you don't measure (he owed me one), it will come back to you times ten.

❑ 89. *If it wouldn't make your mom proud, don't do it.* Take pride in yourself, your company, and what you do. Be an ambassador at all times.

❑ 90. *Never force the sale.* It usually turns out to be a big hassle and a mistake.

❑ 91. *Stay physically fit.* It will improve your performance by 20 percent.

92. *Earn unsolicited referrals on a regular basis.* Ask yourself, "Have I done what it takes so this person will refer me to someone else?"

93. *Do it passionately.* Do it the best it's ever been done. Give the best effort you have—every day.

94. *Be memorable. In a creative way.* In a positive way. In a professional way. What will they say about you when you leave? You are responsible for the memory you leave.

❑ 95. *Resign your position as general manager of the universe.* Before you tackle everyone else's problems, solve your own. Butt out.

❑ 96. *Get great at everything you do.* Be known as the best.

❑ 97. *Speak in public.* It will help you improve presentation skills and position you as an expert. Join Toastmasters Int'l.

❑ 98. *Get involved in your community.* Give back a portion of what is provided to you.

❑ 99. *Find mentors and use them.* If you have desire to succeed, others will help you. Just ask.

❑ 100. *The best way to learn to be successful is to hang around successful people.* Hang around with the best salespeople you know. Avoid people who are not.

❑ 101. *The biggest obstacle to your success is you.* You have been given a bag of cement and a bucket of water. You can either build a stepping stone or a stumbling block. The choice is (and always has been) yours.

The 101.5 characteristic is the most important of them all. **Have fun!** You will succeed far greater at something you love to do. Doing something you enjoy will also bring joy to others. Happiness and enthusiasm are contagious.

Following the fundamental rules of Knock Your Socks Off Selling will lead to sales success faster than any other route you could try.

It is our hope that all your appointments are one-call closes that lead to long-term relationships.

Additional Resources

Zemke, Ron. *Delivering Knock Your Socks Off Service,* 2nd edition. New York, AMACOM Books, 1998.

Zemke, Ron. *Tales of Knock Your Socks Off Service*. New York, AMACOM Books, 1998.

Bell, Chip R. *Customers as Partners: Building Relationships that Last*. San Francisco, Berrett-Koehler, 1994.

Cathcart, Jim. *Relationship Selling: The Key to Getting and Keeping Customers*. New York, Berkley Publishing Group, 1990.

Connellan, Tom. *Inside the Magic Kingdom: Seven Keys to Disney's Success*. Austin, Bard Press, 1996.

Gitomer, Jeffrey H. *Customer Satisfaction is Worthless, Customer Loyalty is Priceless.* Austin, Bard Press, 1998.

Gitomer, Jeffrey H. *The Sales Bible.* New York, William Morrow and Co., 1994.

Leeds, Dorothy. *Smart Questions*. New York, Berkley Publishing Group, 1995.

Mackay, Harvey. *Dig Your Well Before You're Thirsty: The Only Networking Book You'll Even Need.* New York, Doubleday Publishing, 1997.

About the Authors

Jeffrey Gitomer is the author of *The Sales Bible* and *Customer Satisfaction is Worthless—Customer Loyalty is Priceless*. President of Charlotte-based Buy/Gitomer, Jeffrey gives seminars, runs annual sales meetings, and conducts training programs on selling and customer service. His syndicated weekly column, "Sales Moves" appears in more than 50 business newspapers and is read by more than 1,500,000 people. He was appointed lifetime editor of *SalesMasterMind*—a monthly sales newsletter that features Jeffrey and sales experts from all over the world. In 1997, Jeffrey was awarded the designation Certified Speaking Professional (CSP) by the National Speakers Association. He can be reached at 704/333-1112 or e-mail to salesman@gitomer.com.

Ron Zemke is the co-author of AMACOM's six-book *Knock Your Socks Off Service* series, the best-selling *Service America*, and 18 other books on management and employee development. He is president of Minneapolis-based Performance Research Associates and has served as senior editor of *TRAINING Magazine* since 1976. In 1974 he was awarded the Mobius Award for professional achievement by the Society of Consumer Affairs Professionals (SOCAP). In 1999 he was awarded the Thomas F. Gilbert Distinguished Professional Achievement Award by the International Society for Performance Improvement (ISPI). Ron regularly speaks to groups around the world on customer retention and earning customer trust. He can be reached at 800/359-2576 or through www.socksoff.com.